PENGUIN BOOKS

## Two Girls, One on Each Knee

'Alan Connor's charming, fascinating history of how the crossword went from a space filler in the back section of an American newspaper to one of the world's most ubiquitous and addictive habits – he estimates that in Britain some 14.7m people do a crossword at least once a week – is the guide you have been waiting for. In a single, gloriously decipherable chapter he lays out with perfect clarity the entire range of rules and devices through which cryptic clues work their magic' Robert Collins, *Sunday Times*

'Connor's scholarly knowledge doesn't stop him extolling the vocabulary of *The Simpsons*. The solution to the title, by the way, is "patella".' Ben Felsenburg, *Metro*

'No crossword addict, be they a compiler or a solver, can ignore it' Alan Taylor, *Herald*

'Connor's book is cleverly constructed around an initial cryptic crossword in which each clue provides the title of a chapter. And each chapter can be read independently of the others. There is something to entertain even the most infrequent dabbler, from a primer on how to actually do a cryptic crossword to the puzzle's famous fans – the Queen, Sepp Blatter and Frank Sinatra among them – and its connections with the trains (one line in the US used to carry dictionaries)' Carl Wilkinson, *Financial Times*

'Delivers fun galore whether you're a doer or a duffer ... *Two Girls, One on Each Knee* consists of a series of short, sparky chapters on topics as various as "Crosswords and detective fiction", "Can machines do crosswords?" and "The many ways of being rude in a crossword" ... And this is also the guiding principle of his book. It favours the byway over the highway, and can never say no to a red herring' Craig Brown, *Mail on Sunday*

'This book shows you, among other things, how speaking aloud unpromising phrases such as "Tooting Carmen" and "Servants Tease" can yield obvious answers, and how sociable the crossword is. Of course, it can be tackled alone, and in *Brief Encounter*, it represents the antithesis of the longed-for romance, but it's also perhaps fun to tackle with two or more heads rather than one' Michael Caines, *The Times Literary Supplement*

'Connor writes with great flair ... it is nice to dip in and out of his entertaining essays' Don Manley, *Church Times*

'It is the relationship between setter and solver, between words and fun which provides the narrative thrust for *Two Girls, One on Each Knee* ... "The experience of reading this book", Connor says in the preamble, "should be equivalent to that of solving a cryptic puzzle..." In fact it is rather better; it does not demand as much of the reader as a good puzzle does of the solver, but it delivers far more of its own accord. It is witty, charming, encyclopaedic and highly readable – and it can be read in any order. Take a chapter or a paragraph, a puzzle or a clue. In each the reader will find something to intrigue and delight' Sandy Balfour, *Spectator*

'A wonderful little book that looks at the fascinating, often baffling world of the cryptic crossword. What connects Bletchley Park and the *Daily Telegraph*? And why should you always start in the bottom right-hand corner? Most of all, it's a celebration of language' Jon Stock, *Daily Telegraph*

## ABOUT THE AUTHOR
Alan Connor writes weekly about crosswords for the *Guardian*. He has contributed pieces about language for the BBC and the *Guardian* and works in radio and television, writing with Charlie Brooker and Sue Perkins. He is the question editor for the BBC quiz show *Only Connect*. His most recent writing was *A Young Doctor's Notebook*, a TV adaptation of Mikhail Bulgakov stories starring Daniel Radcliffe and Jon Hamm.

# Alan Connor
# Two Girls, One on Each Knee

*The Puzzling, Playful World of the Crossword*

PENGUIN BOOKS

PENGUIN BOOKS

Published by the Penguin Group
Penguin Books Ltd, 80 Strand, London WC2R ORL, England
Penguin Group (USA), Inc., 375 Hudson Street, New York, New York 10014, USA
Penguin Group (Canada), 90 Eglinton Avenue East, Suite 700, Toronto, Ontario, Canada M4P 2Y3
(a division of Pearson Penguin Canada Inc.)
Penguin Ireland, 25 St Stephen's Green, Dublin 2, Ireland (a division of Penguin Books Ltd)
Penguin Group (Australia), 707 Collins Street, Melbourne, Victoria 3008, Australia
(a division of Pearson Australia Group Pty Ltd)
Penguin Books India Pvt Ltd, 11 Community Centre, Panchsheel Park, New Delhi – 110 017, India
Penguin Group (NZ), 67 Apollo Drive, Rosedale, Auckland 0632, New Zealand
(a division of Pearson New Zealand Ltd)
Penguin Books (South Africa) (Pty) Ltd, Block D, Rosebank Office Park,
181 Jan Smuts Avenue, Parktown North, Gauteng 2193, South Africa
Penguin Books Ltd, Registered Offices: 80 Strand, London WC2R ORL, England

www.penguin.com

First published by Particular Books 2013
Published in Penguin Books 2014
006

Image credits p. 15 Stiff Records; p. 72 Calendar Puzzles; p. 77 ITV Global /
THE KOBAL COLL ECTION; p. 88 REX / George Konig; p. 109 Raphael Tuck; p. 118 David
Godine; p. 119 Random House; p. 142 Bettmann / CORBIS ; p. 185 THE SIMPSONS ™ & © 2008
Twentieth Century Fox Film Corporation. All Rights Reserved; p. 202 Universal Images Group /
Getty Images; p. 227 REX / ITV; p. 228 News International.
Every effort has been made to contact copyright holders.
All queries should be addressed to the publisher.

Set in 11.5 /15pt Adobe Caslon Pro and Franklin Gothic
Text design Claire Mason / Typeset by Penguin Books
Printed in Great Britain by Clays Ltd, Elcograf S.p.A.

A CIP catalogue record for this book is available from the British Library

978-0-141-97710-2

www.greenpenguin.co.uk

For Raphael

# Preamble

This is a book about having fun with words. Jumbling them, tumbling them, hiding and sneaking them into unexpected places, making riddles, jokes and poetry in the form of crossword clues. A love of crosswords is also a love of language – albeit a love that enjoys seeing the object of its affections toyed with, tickled and flipped upside-down.

Crossword puzzles are a silly, playful way of taking English and making it into a game. And they have been doing so since 21 December 1913, when the world's first crossword appeared in an American newspaper – although lovers of language had been deriving pleasure from wordplay long before then, of course. However, it was the crossword that came to supersede all other puzzles. It has become a cornerstone of almost all newspapers, and, for many, a fondly anticipated daily appointment.

For some time, the puzzle lived in the form of what we might today call the 'concise' crossword, each answer indicated by a simple definition. But when Britain caught on to the appeal of the crossword in the 1920s, a small group of pioneering setters teased it into different forms, most notably the cryptic, in which each definition is hidden inside devious and frolicsome wordplay.

What all crosswords have in common is the pleasure of identifying what the setter is asking for and seeing the answers mesh with each other until the puzzle is finished. For a century, the commuter has whiled away journeys and parents have passed on tips and tricks in the hope that each grid tackled will be correctly filled. Currently, 14.7 million people in the UK do battle with a crossword at least once a week.

In *Two Girls, One on Each Knee*, we'll be looking at the playfulness, the humour and the frustration of the crossword in all its forms, and how the world of the puzzle has overlapped with espionage and humour, current affairs and literature. We'll see fictional crossword encounters, such as Reginald Perrin locked into eternal rivalry with a fellow commuter and Inspector Morse finding inspiration after solving an especially fiendish clue. And we'll see crosswords from the real world: the one which seemed to predict the outcome of a presidential election and the ones which appeared to be giving away the secrets of D-Day.

We'll look at how clues tantalize those who are addicted to puzzles by sending the solver on wild-goose chases, by appearing to be rude when they (most *definitely*) are not and by stubbornly withholding their real meanings until the penny drops.

And we ask questions about the experience of solving: why do some people try to finish crosswords as quickly as possible? Can computers crack cryptic clues? And does wordplay really stave off dementia?

The experience of reading this book should be equivalent to that of solving a cryptic puzzle, taking you on overlapping journeys. As with the clues in a crossword, you can read the book in any order you like. You can, if you like, start at the beginning. Or you can delve in anywhere you fancy the look of and then flick backwards and forwards at your whim. Like crossword clues, the chapters are of different lengths and tones; they cross paths with each other and then proceed in their own directions. And each is followed by a little extra detail (as if in brackets).

The structure is determined by the puzzle you'll find on pp. xii–xiii. Each clue leads, naturally enough, to an answer, and each answer is the title of a chapter – so you should avoid skipping forward immediately if you want to dodge the spoilers. The answers, and those to the clues that crop up along the way, are at the end. The clues are written by the setter known as Araucaria, a retired churchman considered a friend by many solvers who have never met him but who are devoted to his irreverent, humorous style. For me, I am flattered and unduly honoured by the collaboration.

And what about the title? *Two Girls, One on Each Knee* is itself a cryptic clue, and one that has an exalted place in the history of the crossword. But first, how does it work? Well, like all cryptic clues, it has an apparent meaning, or surface reading: it suggests a grandmother and her grandchildren relaxing on Christmas morning – or, less cosily, perhaps a warlord celebrating at a banquet. Put a letter count after the same phrase, though, and the words begin to yield what lies beneath:

**Two girls, one on each knee (7)**

The first two words give you what crossworders call the wordplay; the rest of the clue is the definition. They both lead you to the answer, but by different routes. With wordplay, you do just as it says: play about with the words and see what comes into your mind. (If you're thinking about the names of two girls, you're on the right track.) With the definition: well, it's easy to see what the setter's looking for – once you've got the answer. In this case, it's the medical name for the kneecap:

Two girls          one on each knee

**PAT   ELLA**

**PATELLA**           **PATELLA**

See?

And why is this clue so celebrated? Answer: it was the two-millionth clue written by Roger Squires, who was named in *The Guinness Book of Records* as the world's most prolific crossword setter. It was published in the *Telegraph*

(Cryptic Crossword no. 25,303) on 14 May 2007, and many people say it is their favourite cryptic clue. Roger's clues sum up the playfulness and ingenuity of cryptic solvers and setters and I'm very grateful to him for allowing me to use it as the title. So onwards, to celebrate the centenary of crosswords, and revel in their wit, deceit and mischief.

Are you ready?

# Contents

# Contents

**DOWN**

# Plum

*P. G. Wodehouse and the craze of the crossword*

P. G. Wodehouse knew his crosswords. We see that in his story 'Summer Moonshine': Lady Abbott, shoeless on the settee, regretfully rejects IRVING BERLIN as a nine-letter answer for an Italian composer beginning with a P 'because, despite his other merits, too numerous to mention here, he had twelve letters, began with an I, and was not an Italian composer'. Her technique is familiar to any solver who has tried, against all the evidence provided by grid, clues and crossing letters, to make a possible answer work. Luckily for Lady Abbott, her husband soon bursts in, scans the newspaper and ...

> [bringing] to the problem the full force of his intellect,
> he took the pencil and in a firm hand wrote down the

word 'Pagliacci'. Each helping each, was the way Sir
Buckstone looked at it.

Never mind that **PAGLIACCI** is an opera, not a composer:
this is a touching and true portrayal of the dual solve,
husband and wife complementing each other in pursuit of
a filled grid.

It's no surprise that Wodehouse adored crosswords –
like his stories, they consist of language pared down to an
elegant minimum and assembled, jigsaw-like, to a
symmetric whole, all to no higher purpose than whiling
away some time and raising a few smiles. It's a pity he
never constructed a whole puzzle, but his stories abound
in clues – and in real life, Wodehouse was, at least initially,
no slouch as a solver. 'When he got the *Times*,' his
grandson recalled, 'he could do the crossword instantly,
filling the answers in as if he was writing a letter.' But the
crosswords Wodehouse preferred were the early puzzles,
which consisted purely of definitions, rather than the
more elaborate wordplay that was to emerge in Britain in
the early thirties.

In the twenties, when crosswords first took off,
Wodehouse was living in the country of their creation [SEE
3 DOWN]. He later recalled a conversation about America
and how 'they're getting pretty nutty in this adopted land
of mine,' citing novelties such as loudspeakers on golf
courses and commenting that:

> The crossword puzzle craze is now at such a pitch, my
> paper informs me, that a Pittsburgh pastor is handing

out crossword slips which, when solved, give the text of
his sermon. They're all loony.

Soon, however, Wodehouse was himself going nutty for
crosswords. It may seem strange now, when crosswords are
an unremarkable part of everyday life, but when the
puzzles first appeared in fiction they were a seriously
contemporary detail. Wodehouse first mentions them, in
passing, in the *Strand* magazine in 1925. In the story 'High
Stakes', Bradbury Fisher annoys his rival J. Gladstone Bott
by getting a place on the crossword team of Sing-Sing
prison – which also boasts such non-penitential activities
as a glee club and a baseball nine.

That year, crosswords had infiltrated almost all of
American culture, providing checkerboard patterns for
dresses, and songs such as 'Cross Words between my
Sweetie and Me' by the Little Ramblers and 'Crossword
Mama, You're Puzzling Me' by Papalia and His Orchestra,
not to mention 'Cross Word Papa (You Sure Puzzle Me)'
by Josie Miles. The storytellers of the twenties used
puzzles for plot as well as for detail: in 1925 Harold Lloyd
is introduced to love interest Peggy in *The Freshman* in a
scene where they peer at 'number 19 vertical – a name for
the one you love', and the two are soon billing
SWEETHEART and cooing HONEYBUNCH to each other as
they attempt to solve the clue, and so true love is born.
Wodehouse was thinking on similar lines in 'The Truth
about George'. Nervous, stammering George Mulliner is
always looking in at the vicarage to ask the lovely Susan
Blake for help with crosswords ...

and Susan was just as constant a caller at George's cosy little cottage – being frequently stumped, as girls will be, by words of eight letters signifying 'largely used in the manufacture of poppet-valves'.

Wodehouse is providing gentle observational humour about the specialist terminology demanded of solvers, but it's also a plot device to bring together two shy individuals. It is not until Susan helps George 'out of a tight place with the word "disestablishmentarianism"' that he realizes she is 'precious, beloved, darling, much-loved, highly esteemed or valued' to him. Here, as in *The Freshman*, the crossword – often characterized as a source of solitary torment – is Cupid, in stark contrast to the film *Brief Encounter*, where the *Times* puzzle almost wrecks a marriage [SEE 17 ACROSS].

By the thirties, the craze was less fervid, and crosswords were as commonplace and contemporary as Wodehouse's slang. Puzzles became not merely something for his characters to do but a way to tell us a little of their personalities. Take George's first cousin once removed, Mervyn Mulliner in 'The Knightly Quest of Merlyn'. When he is at a loss for the name of a large Australian bird beginning with E and ending with U, he 'places the matter in the hands of the editor of the *Encyclopædia Britannica*'.

Mervyn's habit of delegating later lands him in the hot water that gives the novel its title via a subplot involving out-of-season strawberries (of course). Meanwhile, in 'The Code of the Woosters', Madeline Bassett in a moment of apparent inspiration looks at Bertie 'like someone who has

just solved the crossword puzzle with a shrewd "Emu" in
the top right-hand corner'. Crossword emus make many
appearances in Wodehouse stories; indeed, part of the
pleasure of early crosswords and Wodehouse stories is the
variation on familiar subjects: in crosswords, those words
which occur frequently, such as ALOE, ELI and ALAMO [SEE
28 ACROSS]; in Wodehouse, aunts, wagers and
engagements.

The thirties are the golden age for crosswords in
Wodehouse. The *Times* had begun publishing a puzzle in
1930; there, and in the *Observer* and the *Listener*
magazine, the cryptic form was developing and his
characters were beginning to tackle more challenging
clues, in which the definitions are helped or hindered by
such wordplay as anagrams and acrostics. Wodehouse,
too, tried to keep up – indeed, in his correspondence, he
seems more interested in the puzzles than in the news
part of the newspaper, and was even prompted to join a
lively debate on the *Times* letters pages about one of
them. On 17 August 1934 the MP Austen Chamberlain
wrote to boast of finishing that paper's puzzle in forty-
one minutes [SEE 5 DOWN], adding that the Provost of
Eton 'measures the time required for boiling his breakfast
egg by that needed for the solution of your daily
crossword – and he hates a hard-boiled egg'.

The implausible speed of that provost – better known
today as the ghost-story writer M. R. James – galled
Wodehouse, who wrote his own letter five days later to
convey the pleasurable frustration felt by solvers then and
since:

Sir,-On behalf of the great race of rabbits, those humble strivers who, like myself, have never yet succeeded in solving an entire *Times* crossword puzzle, I strongly resent these Austen Chamberlains and what not flaunting their skill in your columns. Rubbing salt in the wounds is what I call it. To a man who has been beating his head against the wall for twenty minutes over a single anagram it is g. and wormwood to read a statement like that one about the Provost of Eton and the eggs. In conclusion, may I commend your public spirit in putting the good old emu back into circulation again as you did a few days ago? We of the *canaille*, now that the Sun-God Ra has apparently retired from active work, are intensely grateful for an occasional emu.

'Canaille', by the way, means the 'vile herd' – it's a self-consciously French way of referring to the lower orders, which pretty much collapses if you try to use it to describe yourself. Wodehouse is making a plea for more of what the creators of puzzles call 'crosswordese' – the old chestnuts that keep returning in grid after grid.

By common consent, greater problems than twenty-minute anagrams awaited Wodehouse as the thirties turned into the forties. The start of the Second World War found the author in Le Touquet in France, and he spent much of the early forties in internment camps, and then in Berlin, where he made some radio broadcasts to reassure his fans that he was alive and well.

The decision to broadcast on Nazi shortwave radio was not popular, however, and was regarded in England and

America as at worst treasonous and at best what Bertie Wooster's Aunt Dahlia would describe as the action of a congenital idiot who 'wants a nurse to lead him by the hand and some strong attendant to kick him regularly at intervals of a quarter of an hour'.

His wartime letters reveal a Wodehouse anxious less about world affairs than about how the Dulwich College cricket team is faring and how soon after publication he's able to get the *Times*. 'I have been able to resume my *Times* crossword puzzles,' he writes to the novelist Denis MacKail in February 1945. 'What is "Exclaim when the twine gives out" in ten letters?'

But even crosswords are offering less comfort as the war goes on. By May, he writes:

> I have finally and definitely given up the *Times* crossword puzzles. The humiliation of only being able to fill in about three words each day was too much for me. I am hoping that what has happened is that they have got much more difficult, but I have a gloomy feeling that it is my brain that has gone back.

Given up? He had. It wasn't the same in the post-war stories. No more firm hands writing **PAGLIACCI**, no poppet-valves acting as Valentines. Aunts lick their pencils in vain frustration and in 'Sticky Wicket at Blandings' Gally Threepwood lights a cigar and looks at the *Times* but finds that 'these crossword puzzles had become so abstruse nowadays and he was basically a Sun-god-Ra and Large-Australian-bird-emu man.' For a while, a butler can be relied upon to shimmy into view and solve the more challenging clues, but in 1957's 'Something Fishy', the clues are left unanswered. From an author whose stock in trade is the relief of tensions and solving of mysteries, the effect is eerie – and the experience, like when you can't finish a real-world crossword, unusually frustrating.

# Other famous solvers

**The Queen,** who begins each morning with the *Telegraph* crossword, accompanied by kippers or kidneys on toast.

**W. H. Auden,** who, when he lived in America, complained about the *New York Times* crossword, which 'frequently drives me up the wall with rage because of the lack of precision in its clues. The clues in British crosswords may be more complicated, but they are always fair.'

**Sepp Blatter,** for whom *The Ultimate Crossword Book* is 'a constant companion'.

**Ian McCulloch** of Echo and the Bunnymen: 'I'm particularly into the cryptic crossword in the *Guardian* – some days it flies, but there are times when I can't finish it because the compiler's put in some sodding historical Egyptian shite.'

**Indira Gandhi,** whose participation in a bilateral economic cooperation agreement is attributed by diplomat and champion solver Roy Dean to

*cont'd*

an ice-breaking conversation about crosswords beforehand.

**Frank Sinatra,** who wrote a fan letter to the *New York Times* puzzle editor giving his solving times, remarking 'What a wonderful way to pass the time and also learn new answers every day.'

**Brenda Blethyn,** who races her brother to complete the cryptics at the *Times* Crossword Club site.

**Norman Mailer,** who told *Newsweek* in 2003 that 'this is how I comb my brain every morning', adding, 'I'm hurt that I'm never in one of them. And I've got a last name with three vowels. You'd think I'd be hot cakes, but I'm not.'

**George VI,** whose last act before dying of a heart attack in his sleep was a late-evening crossword solve.

# Railwaymen

*A century of solving on the train*

From its birth, the crossword has been strongly identified with its older cousin in modernity, the train. Before the age of the paperback, the crossword was the best way of passing some time sitting in a rail carriage. In Colin Dexter's whodunit *The Wench is Dead*, Inspector Morse [SEE 18 DOWN] buys a couple of papers at Oxford railway station and has solved every clue but one in the *Times* before his train reaches Didcot. Lacking 'his faithful *Chambers*' dictionary, Morse fills the empty cells with any old letters, 'in case any of his fellow-passengers were waiting to be impressed'.

If only Morse had been solving during the American crossword boom of the twenties. So engaged were

Americans by the new pastime of crosswording that the Baltimore and Ohio railroad furnished its mainline trains with dictionaries – though these would not have had the range of Scottish and obsolete poetic spellings that makes *Chambers* both a thicker tome and the one most beloved of setters and solvers in search of elusive fish such as the **ID**. And the Pennsylvania Railroad went one better than the B&O, printing crosswords on the menus in the dining car.

For those who want to time their solve [**SEE 5 DOWN**], the journey offers a stopwatch of sorts in its regularity. A *Times* reader once wrote of her father returning home and announcing, 'Ah, it was a tough one today, took me between Barming and Swanley to complete.' That's six stops: East Malling, West Malling, Borough Green & Wrotham, Kemsing, Otford and Swanley, so Dad was clearly no mere dabbler.

As the provision of dictionaries without fear of theft suggests, the passenger who solved was, for a generation or so, a respectable figure. The archetype in England is familiar: pinstripe suit, bowler hat, broadsheet newspaper with crossword.

And if he had travelled in thirties England, Morse need not have struggled alone with that last clue. A solver described the collaboration that took place in first-class carriages at that time:

> The team spirit is essential. There are the centre-forward, the outside-right who is an expert in modern literature, anagrams and farming terms and the outside-left who is only included because he buys the

paper. We could do with a fourth member who can
recite the whole of Shakespeare.

Sadly, the idyll was not to last. In a sketch from *Beryl Reid
Says Good Evening* (1968), Reid plays an uncouth woman
who blunders into the sanctum of stockbroker-belt
commuters and solves the clues that have defeated the
bowler hats, such as 'Rhetorical ninth (10)'. 'Polyhymnia,'
she barks. 'One of the nine muses. Rhetoric, like it says.
Strewth, I thought everybody'd 'eard of 'er. 'Ere, is that the
junior crossword you're doing?'
 Watching the sketch nowadays, it's difficult to recreate
the sense of irony in Reid outwitting the City types. We do
not expect today's captains of industry to be respectably
familiar with the goddesses of the liberal arts, but in the late
sixties the exchange reflected the times in conveying how
the clubby clique of the season-ticket holder was no longer
immune to the lower orders.
 Not that they were known as season-ticket holders any
longer. As of the fifties, the decorous nineteenth-century
term was being superseded by 'commuter'. A season ticket
might have been an establishment badge, but anyone
could be a commuter. The change is apt: from a phrase
describing something you own to one denoting something
you have to do.
 In the sixties, too, the trains themselves began to
change: fewer carriages with corridors leading into snug,
quiet compartments and more saloon coaches with
passengers unseparated by walls. More democratic,
certainly, but less amenable to a group solve. Team spirit

was on the wane, in any event. In 1958 a *Times* reader expressed a wish that each puzzle should be accompanied by the injunction: 'Warning. Clues and answers should not be discussed in public.'

This is the world that Morse was more familiar with: every solver for himself. But it was more than that. Now, you weren't just solving solo; you were in competition with anyone else on the train in possession of the same paper. In David Nobbs' novel *The Fall and Rise of Reginald Perrin*, our beleaguered hero is in perpetual conflict on the 8.16 with Peter Cartwright, who announces, 'Finished!' by Raynes Park while Reggie struggles all the way to Waterloo. Until one day, when Reggie abandons solving proper and lets his frustration spill into the grid, writing in its squares: 'I am not a mere tool of the capitalist society.'

> He folded the paper up and put it in his briefcase.
> 'Rather easy today,' he said.
> 'Damned if I think so,' said Peter Cartwright.

'Could a man,' wonders Perrin, 'go through such an internal struggle and reveal nothing of it in his face?' Work, like the journey to and from the workplace, is, by the time of Perrin – the mid to late seventies – a prison, and the crossword a means of staving off psychic collapse.

Or, in the case of the 1982 Madness single 'Cardiac Arrest', physical collapse. Ten minutes from his stop, the sad hero of this song has still not finished his puzzle. He reflects on how much more difficult the crossword seems to have become recently and how much less pleasure it is affording.

ACROSS:

1) A bowler is a type of... (3)
4) Camden lunacy keeps Stiff people sane (7)
6) Break up the red beds and see a bass guitarist (7)
8) American soldier (2)
9) Sue gets disturbed but finds she's not without some purpose. (3)
10) Chaps, disquieted, leave a singer and trumpet-player (4)
11) Top of the milk after the South reveals a high-pitched shout (6).
12) Was about to discover something to play a tune or help a handyman. (3)
15) Boars running about to find the man who tinkles the ivories. (5)
17) Guitarist with 4 across (7,3)
19) Morse code request for help. (3)
20) Eel does a U-turn and finds a sax maniac. (3)

DOWN:

2) I bail confused to prove that I was somewhere else (5)
3) T. carries a card. (anagram 7,6)
5) Number of sins about event. (5)
7) Singer with 4 across. (5)
8) Blondie's heart, where Kim spilt water and Alice went through. (5)
10) Endless care leads to something you drive around in. (3)
13) Drummer describing an oak or an elm. (5)
14) Five fivers on a little horse. (4)
15) Tweeters out of the speakers. (5)
16) Highest cards from decapitated faces. (4)
18) Love the North East, a step beyond. (3)

However, it's not that his crossword is getting harder, it's that the commuter is exhausted. The crossword can even act as a health warning, with one in-song clue hinting at an imminent **CARDIAC ARREST**. In the eighties, the crossword had lost its role in popular culture as a mark of intellect, signifying instead mental incarceration.

Since then, the terminology has changed again. Passengers have become 'customers' in the grim mercenary vocabulary of 'revenue protectors' and 'Thank you for choosing's, which betrays a change in relationship: the onus is no longer on the train operator to guarantee your passage, it is on you to pony up. Onboard dictionaries are unimaginable on trains whose loos have unbreakable mirrors and unstealable soap –

both of which send the insidious and inescapable message that the operator thinks that, given the chance, you would trash the facilities.

The commuter's experience on a modern train might seem one more of entrapment than in those heady days of post-industrial liberation, where trains seemed to be carrying their passengers to a brighter, better future, but even a penal ambience can't quash the crossword habit. Consider the teenage Stephen Fry, on remand in Pucklechurch young offenders' institute for credit card fraud and finding solace in the *Times* puzzles that his mother cut out of the paper and passed to him under the glass in the visiting room. Better still, consider the setting career of the journalist and novelist Anthony Grey, who created crosswords for *Games and Puzzles* magazine. Grey taught himself how to write cryptic clues in the late sixties when, as a Reuters correspondent, he was jailed by the Chinese authorities and put into solitary confinement:

> As I walked back and forth in the yard later in the day I occupied my mind working out clues ... It allowed me to forget the watching eyes of the guards, occupied my mind, eased the tension in me as I walked.

Now there's a stoicism that puts to shame most niggles about wanting to get on with your puzzle. The next time you bristle at the suspicion that a fellow passenger is peering at your grid, think of Grey, approximate if you can the stiffness of his upper lip – and be thankful.

# Comic clues

In a much-loved *Two Ronnies* sketch set on a train, upper-crust commuter Barker is attempting the Mephistopheles crossword in the *Financial Times* and becomes increasingly irritated by a plebeian Corbett reading aloud a selection of clues from 'the *Sun* Junior Coffee-Time Easy Clues' version and offering his off-beam suggestions for the answers. For 'They peck holes in your milk-bottle tops' with the letters — —TS, he has BATS; for 'It's red, it smells and is often picked in the garden' with —OSE, he has NOSE; and for a fourletter word for 'Place where fish are kept', he has COOP (the Co-Op).

Crosswords are a comic staple of the twentieth century. Workplace sitcom *The Smoking Room* follows the Ronnies in deriving humour from bad solving: the hapless Barry enters THAILAND for 'Home to famous birdman (8)' and BONTEMPI for 'Internal organ (8)', because 'you can play those indoors.'

Other comedies parody crosswords themselves. In *Cheers*, Carla insists that she takes the *National*

*cont'd*

*Inquirer* because 'they happen to have a great crossword puzzle,' which turns out to share the paper's editorial concerns. She rattles with barely a pause through 'Five-headed cow born in Vermont' (**MAYBELLE**), 'State with the most UFO babies' (**ARKANSAS**), 'Aphrodisiac found in every kitchen cabinet' (**OREGANO**) and 'Where Franco's brain is being kept alive' (**FISH TANK**).

And when it comes to cryptics, the humour is in their apparent impenetrability, as when Victor Meldrew tries to relax with a puzzle in *One Foot in the Grave*. Defeated by the clues 'Mad poet mugged by banjo player sees red when eating pickles', 'Bag eggnog but get a tad bugged' and 'Elk's ego gets my goat – head of MI5 upset the French by reversing into Dad's underpants – it's a doddle', he barks, 'I'm sorry. I don't seem to be able to do the crossword today as I appear to be temporarily out of mind-bending drugs.'

# Strong

*The world's most extreme cryptic crossword*
– the Listener

During the writing of *West Side Story* in the midfifties, there was a predictable weekly drop in the productivity of lyricist Stephen Sondheim and composer Leonard Bernstein. The reason was Sondheim's habit of picking up a copy of a British weekly magazine called the *Listener* every Thursday on his way to meet his colleague. He bought it for the crossword. 'I got Leonard Bernstein hooked,' he remembered. 'Thursday afternoons, no work got done on *West Side Story*. We were doing the puzzle.'

Half a century on, the *Listener* magazine is gone, but its crossword continues to grip solvers' minds. You may have seen it in passing one Saturday in the *Times*: it's one of those weekend puzzles that looks quite different to the weekday crosswords. Gone are the familiar symmetrical black squares; instead, there's a grid that is, terrifyingly, mostly in white, the entries divided by little bars, and there's an enigmatic blurb printed next to it. Sometimes, the grid isn't even square. Ye gods! Here, you may think, be crosswording dragons.

But there's no need to hasten away – assuming, that is, you have some time to spare. And not just an hour; more like an afternoon, maybe more. The *Listener* is extreme crosswording all right, but the clue-solving and grid-filling are often not the most important parts of the puzzle. The most important part of the puzzle is figuring out what the challenge is actually going to be. The *Listener*

puzzle isn't just a harder version of your common-or-
garden crossword, it's a different beast entirely: relentless,
ingenious, impossible to ignore.

The *Listener* crossword has been the subject of an
early-day motion in parliament and is the only puzzle
series to have been parodied in *Punch* and by *Not the Nine
O'Clock News*. It's also the only crossword which has
required solvers to cut the completed grid into an origami
wren, an advent calendar or a snowflake – just three
wintry examples – and what's more, this nonsense has
been going on for three quarters of a century.

In 1929 BBC Director-General Lord Reith established
the *Listener* magazine as an erudite partner to the *Radio
Times*, to provide easy access to highbrow, often
modernist, ideas. Contributors were to include Virginia
Woolf, T. S. Eliot and an eighteen-year-old Philip Larkin.
If you listened to the BBC's better broadcasts and read the
*Listener*, you could consider yourself plugged in to the
cultural and occasionally bohemian life of the nation. On
2 April 1930 – before the conventions of the cryptic were
fully established [SEE 17 DOWN] – the magazine began to
run a crossword, offering as a prize 'an invitation to visit
the B.B.C. Studios on certain afternoons'. Only one
correct solution was received, from a Mr I. Cresswell of
Colchester; some later puzzles would receive none.

Not much is known of those who edited the puzzle.
These anonymous pioneers were learning on the hoof
about what the crossword was capable of, and were
sometimes game enough to share the experience in the

magazine's correspondence pages. To this day, the *Listener* is unlike weekday crosswords: while it is open to all to enter and its editors are now named, much less is known about its setters, who often appear just once, with a puzzle of mephistophelean intricacy, and then vanish in a puff of sulphurous smoke.

*Listener* 1 was headed 'A Musical Crossword' and initiated a tradition of themed and titled puzzles. Subsequent issues included, from a variety of setters, A Scientific Crossword, A Botanical Crossword and, intimidatingly, A Latin Crossword. Did this last test your knowledge of a dead language? Of course – and An Indian Crossword, which had a grid in the shape of the subcontinent, asked you to draw on your knowledge of Hindustani.

Nowadays, the themes are less daunting: you're more likely to meet Hitchcock or the Hadron Collider than you are Hindi dialects, but the use of themes and titles persists. The main difference is that the title no longer reveals the theme; in fact, the gradual emergence of the secret structure of a *Listener* puzzle is the second-best thing about solving it.

The *best* thing is that penny-drop moment when the solver realizes that the completed grid is not merely an arrangement of the answers to the clues but a crafty illustration of something else: a map of the Glasgow underground system, a game of Space Invaders or a representation of a Kipling poem. The clues and the filling of the grid – there is, at least, almost always a grid in *Listener* puzzles – are there initially to hide and later reveal what the puzzle is really depicting.

Take my first experience of tackling the *Listener*. Its

author was Sabre and its title was 'Author'. That confusion
was nothing compared to what was to follow.

The puzzle concealed the title of a Sherlock Holmes
story in its clues. Co-solving with a friend, we read the
story for further clues: in it, Holmes pontificated on a
fictional book code in which numbers indicate words in a
certain text. But it didn't stop there. The endgame was a
real-world book code which had as its text another
Holmes tale. Decrypting this tortuously revealed an
instruction to write certain letters from the answers 'in
scarlet'. To what end? The name **MORIARTY** emerged
across the grid, and this in itself pulled together the last
loose strands of Sabre's devious construction.

The experience was exhausting, audaciously demanding
and as much fun as I've ever had with a crossword – and
while it's at the more involving end of the spectrum, it's a
wholly representative introduction to the quirks and joys
of the *Listener* puzzle: in particular, the importance of
scrutinizing the preamble for hints as to what could
possibly be going on.

The preamble often tells you how the 'entry' (what you
write in the grid) differs from the 'answer' (what the clue
indicates). You might be adding letters, you might be
removing letters, you might be writing some answers in
backwards … anything goes.

The gimmicks are not there merely for the challenge of
having multiple interpretations of a single clue, however:
they form part of a holistic whole of puzzlement.

The other thing that is notable about the *Listener*

crossword is the sometimes bizarre vocabulary or aberrant spelling of some of its clues, which, again, is for good reason. The preamble always ends by recommending the *Chambers* dictionary, beloved of compilers for its inclusion of wayward spellings of familiar words from the likes of Shakespeare and Spenser and terminology from around the UK and/or olden times. This means a little digging around to see whether DROUGHT can be rendered DROUTH in Scotland (it can), but also means that setters have much more scope to arrange a completed grid such that, say, the letters THE GRAND CANAL snake through the middle in the shape of Venice's waterway and other parts can be shaded to make a map of the city-state and its islands. (The barred grid also means that crossing letters start to appear much more quickly than in a blocked puzzle, making guessing words like DROUTH a little easier.)

Once the grid starts to fill, the endgame approaches, and even if the solver has made use of a digital version of a dictionary to help find the more obscure words [SEE 19 ACROSS], no shortcuts are now available. He or she peers at the message revealed by misprints in the definitions of the down clues, or scans the grid for the name of an author in the diagonals: at this point, it's a matter of putting in the perspiration until the moment of inspiration. Other times, the endgame involves trial-and-error construction, as in Quinapalus's 1997 puzzle Brick Wall, in which the entries took the form of Tetris bricks and had to be assembled to create a gapless wall.

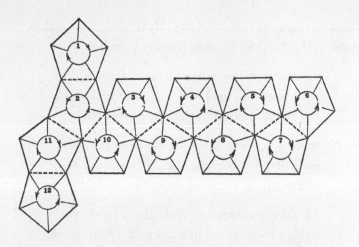

# Dodecahedron *by Jeffec*

The diagram forms a regular twelve-sided solid when folded along the dotted lines. The clues in Group A lead to words of six letters; each of these words contains all the (mixed) letters of a 5-letter word, clued in Group B, plus one extra letter. The extra letters are to be entered in the centres of the appropriate pentagons with the associated 5-letter words inscribed round them (to read in the directions shown by the arrows) so that at each edge of the solid adjacent letters are the same. When the diagram is complete the central letters spell out what lucky geometricians do. Ignore punctuation.

GROUP A – **1.** We the disciples swallowed an insipid Scottish dish **2.** Half a dozen spots not in the avenues **3.** In a manner of speaking violin follows fashion **4.** Casts found in members of the government **5.** In Edinburgh a hired mourner's given gold to pass the night **6.** Take broken lever outside Hodge's metal ring **7.** Vex the old block **8.** Terrier, perhaps, who is disloyal **9.** He seeks to gain gold by Spenser's chase **10.** Waist-belt for East German in nearly zero surroundings **11.** Vexes the Norse god in the river **12.** Great society battles

GROUP B – **a.** To govern in Scotland, be active, move around **b.** Posts of authority: they support the capitals **c.** Show one to be absent in the festival **d.** You with me on hill ridge **e.** Pole might wound to rob: that's the point **f.** In the Great Lakes it swims towards a fiddle of primitive tone **g.** Handle menace: expel hydrogen **h.** With drink about is for movement between the pillars **j.** Recognizes smells – of rhinos especially **k.** Squadron's heading in tanks for the wide open spaces **m.** Race in the northern tide? That's strictly for the birds! **n.** Keeping esteem in abundance, as before

*Listener* endgames have included (NB: these are spoilers if you're in the habit of tackling vintage puzzles):

// shading every instance of the letters N–Z in the completed grid to reveal a 'normal' blocked crossword hidden in the one just solved

// writing the letters upside-down or sideways, such that 'E's become 'M's, 'C's become 'U's, and so on

// a hidden message which leads to another hidden message … not quite ad infinitum, the final instruction being to draw the sign for infinity in the completed grid

// removing the names of German children (MAX, OTTO, ELSA, etc) from answers and making them 'follow' the words PIED PIPER 'out' of the puzzle

// making knight's moves across the surfaces of a cube to mark the Queen's Silver Jubilee

// deciphering hidden messages in Morse code to produce in the grid a representation of Beethoven's Fifth (V being *dit-dit-dit-dahhhhh* in Morse)

// treating the rows as lines on a musical stave and picking out a tune

… and there will be more. Setters are still finding new arrangements of real-world squares and rectangles – from

Battenberg cakes and Noughts and Crosses to paving stones and snooker tables – as inspiration for their grids. Others rely on mathematical problems (the solver is not expected to have maths beyond GCSE level but is expected to think laterally) or inventive ways of arranging the answers: honeycombs, wheels, and so on. You might expect all the low-hanging fruit to have been picked in the puzzle's first eight decades, but it continues to surprise.

Most puzzles are like separate institutions within the newspapers on which they're printed, and that's especially the case with the *Listener*. Indeed, the puzzle survived its change of host when the *Listener* folded in 1991 and its crossword was adopted by the *Times*. There was a moment of uncertainty six years later when the *Times* wondered about devoting valuable space to a relatively niche feature, but the future first minister of Northern Ireland, Peter Robinson, stepped in.

Moved by a letter from a worried constituent about the *Listener*'s future, he tabled an early-day motion:

> That this House recognizes that the *Listener* Crossword, which appears in the *Times* newspaper every Saturday, (i) is the most challenging and imaginatively devised cryptic crossword currently published in a national newspaper and (ii) gives much pleasure to thousands of devoted solvers; notes with concern that the Editor of the *Times* plans to discontinue this historic crossword from September 1997; and urges him to reconsider his

decision, thereby ensuring that the *Listener* crossword continues to be published well into the next millennium.

And as the millennium came and went, the puzzle was intact. Apocalypse had been averted. Kudos to the *Times* – although the puzzles are edited and entries marked by a team wholly separate from the paper's staff – and 'entries marked' of course means something unique in the case of this puzzle.

Every one sent to the St Albans address printed next to the preamble is examined, and regular solvers receive an annual handwritten list of which puzzles they've successfully completed and what errors they've made in the others. The indefatigability of the people who have been known as the *Listener*'s statisticians is staggering: solvers also discover the most common errors made in a given year, which solvers failed successfully to finish fewer than ten puzzles and a report on the annual dinner to which setters and champion solvers have been invited since 1975.

The community and care around the *Listener* make it even less like a normal weekday puzzle, but solvers who are terrified about the idea of having their work marked and judged against the efforts of others can be reassured that posting a solution is very much an optional extra, albeit one that can become a compulsion. A run of fifty or more all-correct submissions can come later – all you need to start is a Saturday afternoon with nothing to do, a pencil and a copy of *Chambers* – and, depending on where the puzzle takes you, some Sherlock Holmes stories, maybe some coloured pencils, a pair of scissors and some sticky-back plastic …

# How to defeat the *Listener*

Consider the **title**. What is it on about? Probably not the first interpretation that springs to mind, or the second or the third, for that matter. Maybe look it up in *Chambers* to see if it is some obsolete Australian piece of slang.

Read the **preamble**. Read it again. And again. Well, you get the picture. If anything seems unusually phrased, it is probably for a reason. Rest assured that it will eventually make perfect sense, albeit once you've finished the puzzle.

Read the first letters of the clues in case a sneaky **acrostic** is hidden there. Do the same with the last letters of the clues. Sometimes you will later discover that each clue has an extraneous word and that there is a message in, say, the penultimate letters of each, but it would be madness squared to look for this kind of jiggery-pokery at the outset.

Work from a **copy of the grid,** in **pencil.** Even if your entries are correct, you may well be asked to mess about with them later.

Write the **answers** next to the clues in case the entries turn out to require modification and you later realize that you have utterly forgotten what the original words ever were.

*cont'd*

If further instructions are spelled out by misprints or superfluous words, start looking early for **helpful words** such as **LETTERS**, **WORDS**, **CLUES**, **HIGHLIGHT**, **ACROSS** and **DOWN**. This is not only the point where you realize that George Washington, say, and his tree are concealed in the grid, it also might help identify the misprints, etc, you haven't yet spotted. Likewise, as the grid fills, look in the **diagonals** and around the **perimeter** for any concealed theme words or messages.

When looking for a theme, scan the areas of the grid with the most **bars**: thematic material is more likely to be spread across words than within them. Also, don't assume that you're looking for something in so conventional a form as normal English: it may be a Latin quote, or a chess problem.

Also scour the areas surrounding any place names, surnames or other **vocabulary not found in** *Chambers*: the setter may have been forced to use a non-dictionary word to help spell out the thematic material.

If you're stuck on what the theme might be, look up **anniversaries** in the week of publication. Ten years ago, or a hundred, or, in the case of the Authorized Version of the Bible, four hundred …

Revelation of the theme should be accompanied by an audible sigh or 'Aha'. You'll know when you've got it: if the answer doesn't seem completely right, it isn't.

# 11

# Affronts

*Topics that are best avoided in puzzles*

I got a letter from an eight-year-old boy complaining that while he'd found that the only answer that fitted was 'wooden leg', as a reader of Moby-Dick he knew that Captain Ahab had an ivory leg. Perfectly true, but I couldn't help wondering, rather testily, what an eight-year-old was doing reading Moby-Dick.

— Margaret Farrar, former crossword checker for the *New York World*

The world's first ever complaint about a crossword came when the paper which first ran a puzzle [SEE 3 DOWN] omitted to print it one Sunday. 'The only thing I give a hang about on your page or in your Sunday magazine,' wrote a distraught solver to the *New York World*, 'is the cross-word puzzle.'

By the 1990s, *Times* solvers were more playfully philosophical when a puzzle was printed with a grid that didn't match the clues – five boasted that they had worked out the correct arrangement of squares and solved it anyway. A further five added, in comments paraphrased by the puzzle's upset setter Bob Bartholomew, 'What a splendid idea, you should repeat this kind of challenge from time to time!'

In 2008, when the *Guardian* printed the wrong grid, helpful solvers said they were quite sure that new technology could remedy the oversight at speed, one asking for the correct arrangement of squares by email ('Speedy response appreciated, my lunch break ends at 13.30.').

Solvers in general, though, have signed up for a certain degree of frustration in tackling a crossword at all and are understandably reluctant to have any non-solving frustration added to their challenge. The easiest way to infuriate solvers is to make it impossible for them to find the puzzle; failing that, to move it somewhere unexpected. When the *Guardian* was redesigned in 1997, someone came up with the bright idea of putting the quick crossword on the same page as the cryptic. 'The resulting telephone calls, letters and emails,' wrote crossword editor Hugh Stephenson, 'far outnumbered all those on other aspects of the redesign put together.' Households had become accustomed to being able to allocate the main section to the solver of the 15-by-15 challenge while

someone else took the second section for a simpler puzzle,
and readers 'found themselves fighting turf wars over the
same section or, worse, tearing it in two'.

Even the puzzle that is in its proper place has to tread
carefully. In 1966 Margaret Farrar, who had overseen that
first puzzle series in the *New York World* [SEE 3 DOWN] and
went on to become the first *New York Times* crossword
editor, told the sixteen-year-old would-be setter Merl
Reagle that 'crosswords are entertainment', advising him
to avoid 'things like death, disease, war and taxes – the
subway solver gets enough of that in the rest of the paper.'
Forty years later, Reagle, by then an established setter,
reflected on another category: bodily functions. URINE is
an example of a word which would frequently fit with the
letters already in place in a grid but strikes the wrong note.
'Same with ENEMA,' he sighed. 'ENEMA: talk about great
letters!'

And then there's sex. In 2006 *The New York Times* had a
clue that read:

### Scoundrel

Seven letters, the answer SCUMBAG, and there were
complaints from members of the newspaper staff as well
as from readers. The issue was a different, more physical,
sense of 'scum', and the original sense of SCUMBAG: a
condom. For that reason, *The New York Times* tends not to
use the word: when a congressman said of Bill Clinton,
'The guy's a scumbag,' the paper reported the 'use of a
vulgarity for a condom to describe the President'. Its style
guide acknowledges the drawbacks of primness, or rather,

'taking a stand for civility in public discourse, sometimes at an acknowledged cost in the vividness of an article or two'.

To the British, this decorum is bewildering, and it reveals a difference in the attitudes to word games. In America, crosswords are associated with respectability, good behaviour and courtesy: being good with language and being a good citizen. In Britain, where a well-deployed cuss need not impugn the speaker's respectability, it's about playing games with language, almost all of language, including – perhaps especially – the scaggy, scuzzy, scummy bits.

No, to really get under the skin of a British solver, you need to bring to mind not the bedroom but social difference as it is revealed through speech – specifically, through accent. So when the veteran setter Rufus, who can be found in most broadsheets on a Monday under various pseudonyms, writes a soundalike clue such as ...

**US treasury base struggled with pounds, say (4, 4)**

... where one 'says' 'fought knocks' for the answer **FORT KNOX**, he can be sure of causing teeth-gnashing in Scotland, where the **R** in **FORT** is rhotically rolled, making it sound quite distinct from 'fought'. Likewise, beware the setter who suggests that **GARNER** sounds like **GHANA**, that **WAR** sounds like the author **WAUGH**, or indeed that **SHORE** sounds like the writer **SHAW**. What solver wants a puzzle to suggest that he or she has been pronouncing those words 'wrongly'? In American puzzles, by contrast, there is a sense of wilful fun around such homophone clues as

'Book about the writing style of the Mongols?' (**PROSE AND KHANS**.)

Another area all setters would be well advised to avoid is race. The pioneering cryptic setter A. F. Ritchie, headmaster of Wells Cathedral School, laid down conventions for setting which are followed to this day [**SEE 1 DOWN**]. The same cannot be said for his sense of humour, at least as expressed in this clue from the 1940s:

> What do happen, Mose, if our gals lose deir heads?
>   Oh, den you find de ways out! (8)

In the twenty-first century, you'd be staggered to find 'negresses' as an answer or as part of the wordplay, let alone this uncharacteristically ham-fisted attempt to indicate the answer, **EGRESSES**. But as **NEGRESS** and indeed **JEWESS** have passed out of common use, newer imprecations such as 'chav' risk the same charge of insensitivity.

And what of Farrar's death and disease? The *Times*' advice to setters is to avoid 'words with unpleasant or non-drawing-room associations (e.g. leprosy, carcinoma, incontinent)'. Also unsuitable for the drawing room and the Sunday breakfast are unpleasant events, such as the deaths of public figures. The *Telegraph* had the misfortune to clue **BLUE MURDER** as 'Outcry at Tory assassination (4, 6)' in the edition with a front page devoted to the assassination of Conservative MP Ian Gow in 1990.

The clue had been written four months before and, while the security services did not in this instance launch an investigation [**SEE 23 ACROSS**], readers were understandably upset that the crossword, typically a haven from grim reportage, appeared to be making wordplay out of misery. 'I very nearly got fired,' crossword editor Val Gilbert told the BBC in 2008. Likewise, the *Guardian* setter Paul had included **BIN LADEN** in the first week of September 2001. Whoops.

On very rare occasions, unpleasantness is not an accident.

One of the UK's best-loved setters is John Graham, the retired clergyman who sets for the *Guardian* as Araucaria. Early in his crosswording career, he was advised by the paper's puzzle editor which subjects to avoid: 'No diseases, no religion and no Bible ... no advertising, no brand names and not too much by the way of politics.'

Many of these sensibilities have since gone by the wayside: **HOOVER** is as likely to appear as a brand name as it is a politician, but the 'drawing-room' steer on diseases, at least serious ones, is generally heeded. Which made it all the more shocking when Araucaria himself published a puzzle in 2013 with a preamble that began 'Araucaria has 18 down of the 19'. Eighteen down was easy enough:

**Sign of growth (6)**

The solver, expecting nothing unusual, runs through the six-letter signs of the zodiac to find one that can also be indicated by 'growth'. Not **PISCES, TAURUS** or **GEMINI** ... but **CANCER** fits. Then, before even writing in the answer, the penny drops and the stomach lurches, with no way back: Araucaria has **CANCER**. The puzzle was originally published in the December 2012 issue of *1 Across*, the

monthly crossword magazine co-founded by Araucaria in
1984, where it had a longer preamble, which, once you'd
filled the grid, could be decoded as:

> I have CANCER of the OESOPHAGUS; no
> CHEMOTHERAPY, just PALLIATIVE CARE; no
> NARCOTIC or STENT or MACMILLAN NURSE yet
> - plenty of MERRIMENT, though I wouldn't have
> chosen the timing.

Nobody would chastise John Graham for defying the
expectation that solving won't make you feel queasy.
Normally, Araucaria puzzles are known for their wit and
warmth; unusually for the setter, the experience of solving
this puzzle wasn't in the least fun for the solver, though
there was surely pleasure in marvelling at the enormous
chutzpah of responding to such a diagnosis with a themed
puzzle. In crosswords, all rules are eventually broken.

# How to avoid upsetting solvers

Go easy on specialist scientific vocabulary, remembering that your ideal-type solver is a generalist. Not everyone is a particle physicist ...

... but do your best to counter the overwhelming liberal-arts bias in themes and clues. Particle physicists need love too.

Check which century it is: IT has not meant 'Italian vermouth' since the fifties, but is frequently used to indicate 'information technology'.

Be careful with politically sensitive abbreviations, such as 'Ulster' to indicate NI in a clue. As a rule of thumb, if blood has been shed over a device, it is time to rewrite.

Above all, be careful how you describe the movement of amphibians. 'Frogs hop, sir,' wrote a solver to *New York Times* puzzle editor Will Shortz, 'but toads do not. They waddle.'

# 12

# Beginner

*A toolkit for solving cryptic clues*

British crosswords are more or less of two types: the quick, with definitions telling the solver how to fill 13 by 13 squares; and the cryptic, with longer, stranger clues and 15 squares on each side. Of these, the cryptic is the easier. Newcomers tend to regard this claim as hyperbole verging on the delusional and to back away rapidly, protesting that cryptic crosswords demand a special – even an odd – kind of brain.

But, for one thing, the quick has a tendency to bleed into crypticness. It's the same people who set cryptics as set quicks, so it's understandable that they don't restrict themselves to 100 per cent definitions. Anagrams have a place in the quick, especially those which look very different to the answer and need a little time to unscramble. Sometimes the clues have more than one definition, or a playful definition that doesn't quite mean what it says.

Consider a quick clue like 'Flat (4)'. This could be answered by WEAK or DULL ... or even DEAD. Or even EVEN, for that matter. You can't write anything in yet. That's one delay. So not so quick. You look at one of the answers which crosses with the last letter – let's say it's 'Disposition (6)'. Well, you might have some ideas, but it could still be DULL and LAYOUT, or EVEN and NATURE. More hold-ups.

Now imagine that it's a cryptic crossword and each of those entries is clued with a double definition: a clue in two handy, interconnecting parts. Let's say 'Quits flat (4)' and 'Kind disposition (6)'.

There's only one word which fits both halves of the clue once you think of 'quits' not as 'leaves' but in the sense of 'call it quits', and 'flat' not as a dwelling but as in 'flat as a pancake'. For the other, it's 'kind' not as in tender-hearted but as in 'What kind of man is this?' and 'disposition', straightforwardly, as in 'an unfriendly disposition'.

So you can write in EVEN and NATURE without worrying about whether they fit with the other clues. Easier than the quick equivalents, and quicker too – although it would be a shame not to linger for a moment on the pleasing surface reading of each: the concisely expressed image of someone giving up their apartment, or the welcome sight of someone who is going to be nice to you. And these are pretty much as short as cryptic clues get: as you'll see,

longer ones start to tell miniature stories, or present you
with endearingly daffy imagery.

More importantly, you don't have to worry as much
about the grid: you have a sense when you've cracked each
clue, without having to see whether the option you've
chosen is going to mess up the interlocking entries: in a
cryptic, each clue is a miniature puzzle in itself.

If you can see how 'Quits flat' and 'Kind disposition'
work, you've got the hang of the **double definition**. Here
are some more examples. Remember that the answer
might be indicated by, say, a noun in one half of the clue
but by an adjective in the other. (Solutions and setters are
given at the end of the book.)

**Boat put in water (6)**

**Potty train (4)**

**Very exciting, filthy habit (4–6)**

Got them? Now you're ready for the rarer variant: the
triple, quadruple and quintuple definitions:

**Hand over identity card while away (4)**

**Target vessel and ram end (4)**

**Do quickly stop, take away and kill pirate (5, 3)**

That's the essence of cryptic crosswords right there:
splitting the words of the clue into separate parts and
seeing what they suggest. Not so diabolical, is it?

The next weapon in your toolkit is the **cryptic
definition**. In a typical cryptic clue, you find a definition of
the answer at the beginning or the end of the clue; here

you get another one making up the rest, like in the double definitions above – but things are a little more playful.

So, in 'Savagely competitive boxer getting to do more than bite his opponent? (3-3-3)', the first two words are the definition of **DOG-EAT-DOG** and the rest is a more picturesque route to the same destination. Clues with a cryptic definition will sometimes – but by no means always – include a question mark to let you know that fun is being had.

Try some more. If they don't yield, having a look at the answer and working backwards is just as good a way of grasping how it all works.

**Remember Pooh's imaginary? (4, 2, 4)**

**Too old to walk up and down here? (4, 3, 4)**

**Unfathomable, not like A Midsummer Night's Dream (10)**

And once you've got those, remember that setters will occasionally give a clue containing just the cryptic definition part, if it leads to a pleasing surface reading or is likely to raise a smile. It works much like a stand-alone riddle:

**Sole trader? (10)**

**His second mate gets him into trouble (8)**

**Animal tormentors who usually avoid charges (8)**

Now we'll take a step closer to the form taken by almost all other clues: definition plus wordplay. The definition still comes at the beginning or the end of the clue, and the rest is a disguised instruction about how to assemble the letters of the clue. The form of wordplay you might

associate most strongly with cryptic crosswords is the
**anagram,** where the wordplay is normally made up of an
indication that you should be jumbling some letters and
precisely those letters that need jumbling.

That indication could be anything that suggests
change: movement, confusion or even drunkenness. In
'Male injured too, unfortunately, in play (5, 3, 6)',
'unfortunately' is the hint that you need to rearrange the
letters of 'male injured too' to make the title of a play:
ROMEO AND JULIET. And in 'President's unexpected vote
loser (9)', 'unexpected' tells you to scramble 'vote loser' for
President ROOSEVELT.

**Give short change? That's a mistake (9)**

**Strange I should tan poorly (10)**

**Demand to rewrite scenes in it (10)**

Once you've got into the habit of spotting an anagram,
you're ready for some clues where the definition part
bleeds into the rest of the clue:

**Art's model, possibly (3, 6)**

**They observe transport site movements (13)**

**What could produce fir cone? (7)**

Setters have a tendency to see anagrams before other
clueing devices, and most newspapers have a formal or
informal agreement to limit the number of anagrams in a
given puzzle to make for more variety in clueing styles,
though, as *Sunday Times* puzzle editor Barbara Hall noted,

'of course the compilers get around that because we split them up into mini-anagrams'.

More on clues that are split into different mini-parts presently. Our next technique is the **hidden answer**. Here, again, there's a definition at either the beginning or the end of the clue; the rest is made up of a string of words that contain the answer and a hint that this is what's going on.

The pleasure here is in noticing that the answer has been in front of you the whole time, hiding in plain sight. So in 'Some forget to get here for gathering (3-8)', you're being asked to take 'some' of the letters of 'forget to get here' for GET-TOGETHER; and in 'What's in Latin sign, if I can translate, is of no importance (13)', you need to find 'what's in' 'Latin sign, if I can translate': INSIGNIFICANT. Try these:

> As seen in jab, reach of pro miserably failing to meet
>   expectations? (6, 2, 7)
>
> One lewdly desiring some bicycle chains (4)
>
> How some answers may be found in clues, some
>   of which I'd denoted (6)

As the pioneering cryptic setter Afrit [SEE 1 DOWN] wrote, the clue which hides the answer 'may be flagrantly misleading, but the solver cannot complain, because there the solution is, staring him in the face'. Harsh, but fair.

You're ready now for the information that the hidden word might go backwards, which means that, along with the wordplay, the phrase containing the answer and the hint that you need to take part of that phrase, you'll be

given the sense of going backwards (in an across clue) or
upwards (in a down clue):

> Motorcyclist perhaps steered irresponsibly when
> reversing? Not entirely (5)
>
> Cooking equipment taken back from heiress I
> tormented (10)
>
> Up in spare room, I'm editing actress on film (4, 5)

Now that you're thinking about reading letters backwards,
it's time for the **reversal**. Here you find a definition of the
answer; as you must be expecting by now, a hint to
another word; and an instruction to write that one
backwards to find the answer a second time. So 'Return
friends' makeup (4)' is asking you to find a word meaning
'friends' and spell it backwards for a word meaning
'makeup': SLAP. And in the down clue 'Serve up a drink fit
for a king (5)', you write the name of a drink from bottom
to top and find that you have, from top to bottom, REGAL.
See if you're ready to roll:

> Picked stuff that's green and returned bags? (4)
>
> Grass one should put back, and maybe does (4)
>
> Advanced from the right with others (2, 2)

You are now already good enough at decrypting cryptics
to go up a level – with a little help. In the clues below, the
wordplay asks you to reverse a word, and add something
else: in the first two cases, it's the letter A; in the final
one, it's an A and an O (in tennis, 'love' means zero,
which looks like an O). You can if you wish ponder some

of the explanations people have offered down the ages for this odd terminology, especially the one which says that 'love' derives from the French for a zero-shaped item, the egg (*l'oeuf*), or you can just remember that 'love' often means O in crosswords and move on with your solve.

> There's a marked inclination here to knock back a
> drink (4)
>
> Produce picture with a backing that produces
> Oscar, say (5)
>
> A jewel returned after love letter (5)

Once you've got the sense of how those three combine different parts of wordplay – whether you solved them or looked at the answers – you've unlocked the majority of the rest of cryptic clues. Kudos. Either way, that's the toolkit. You know everything the setter does and the playing field has an EVEN NATURE.

Many cryptic crosswords have wordplay that's made of **one thing after another,** so when the setter Quixote asks for 'Student seen as "home bird" (6)', he wants you to take a word for being 'home' (in, as in 'I'll be in all evening') and combine it with a kind of 'bird' (the tern) to make up a student: INTERN. Here are some examples of what are sometimes called 'charades', after the old parlour game. Each has two words to combine for the entry; in the third, they're given in reverse order:

> Players below par no longer wanted (4-3)
>
> Carol thus delivered girls' beach wear (10)
>
> Wine following pudding gives one the shakes later (10)

Next, some words that aren't words. In the clues below,
you're putting one thing after another again, but some of
the elements are abbreviations you might have seen
somewhere in the non-crosswording world, such as C for
'Tory' (as seen on election night after the name of a
Conservative candidate), PS for 'note' (at the end of a
letter), C for 'college' and L for 'Left':

Split of Tory and Socialist (5)

Arm extension from this moment, note (7)

Intellectual seen in college before getting support
by Left (8)

We're in the home straits now. **Abbreviations** such as
those we've just met are an element of cryptic clueing it
can take a while to get your head around. Essentially, if
you can find some single- or double-letter abbreviation in
a dictionary, it's fair game in a crossword. It's really a
question of whether you can imagine seeing that letter
used somewhere to indicate one of the words in a clue:
for example, A on the back of a car means that it's from
Austria; b on a cricket scorecard means bowled; C on a
tap means that it's cold ... if in doubt, it's not cheating
[SEE 19 ACROSS] to check a dictionary. It's not a question
of memorizing a whole set of codes – you get quickly to
the point where you can sniff them lurking in a clue.

Right, two more devices and you should be ready to
solve. Clues which use **soundalikes** give you a definition
at one end or the other, plus a word or phrase and a
suggestion that you conjure up another word or phrase

that sounds the same. 'Excited as Oscar's announced (4)', for instance, asks you to think of a well-known playwright called Oscar and then write in the synonym for 'excited' that sounds the same: WILD. The hint that there's a homophone can be anything that involves speaking or hearing:

> Musical work that's melodious to the ear (5)
>
> Heard no sound from the stable? (5)
>
> Mentioned pet getting soft drinks (5)

Soundalike clues are close to puns and, as such, a matter of taste. The words in question generally do indeed sound alike when expressed in something approaching received pronunciation, but setters will occasionally have some fun by asking you to 'say' a word in your head using an accent [though SEE 11 ACROSS]:

> Big beast sounds little in Scotland (5)
>
> Is it raised by suspicious East End intellectual? (7)
>
> In Belfast picks up an ounce and performs part of baptism? (7)

The last cryptic device we'll look at is the **acrostic**, itself a kind of puzzle that predates the crossword [SEE 6 DOWN]. Here, the wordplay invites you to take the first letters of a run of words in the clue 'Starts to serve time in Russian prison (4)'. 'Starts' indicates that the initial letters of 'serve time in Russian' will give you an anagram for 'prison': STIR. The setter's job is to disguise that this is what's

going on; yours is to spot that and then pluck out those
letters.

**Black and white lamb starts to cry (4)**

**Does he lead prayer for openers? Is Mohammed a
Muslim? (4)**

**Natty, elegant and trim, primarily (4)**

The final twist is that, just as you might sometimes put
one thing after another, other times you put **one thing
inside another**. In these clues, the acrostic part of the
wordplay contains another element, or is contained by it:

**Guest - unusually for starters - grabs a refreshing
cup cake (6)**

**Sadat, possibly capturing leaders of terrorist insurgents,
opposing conflict (4-3)**

**Ratted on man in misery, blocking opening stages of
the divorce (3-5)**

That's it. You're a solver. Go and buy a newspaper or spark
up your web browser. Most of the clues in its puzzle
should yield once you've set about them with the tools
given above. Others may be made up of combinations,
such as a reversal with an anagram – or a clue might do
the opposite of what you expect: an acrostic-type device
which asks you to take the last letters of a string of words,
say, or a related trick, where you 'decapitate' a down clue
and use everything except the first letter. Or there might
be the odd spoonerism [SEE 15 DOWN].

Discovering these variants is much of the fun. All the devices can be combined and twisted to produce surface readings in each clue which point you in the wrong direction. Your job is to enjoy – perhaps with a friend or relative – puzzling out what's really being said. You're welcome.

# All-in-one

A good cryptic clue is a sentence with an apparent meaning that has nothing whatsoever to do with the word or phrase that it is indicating. But a *really* good cryptic clue does exactly the opposite: the definition, rather than hiding, is right out there for all to see, and the wordplay gives you the second route using *exactly the same words*.

On rare and happy occasion, a setter will find such a sentence: one that does both jobs simultaneously. Devotees call these *&lit*s, a name that's not particularly beginner-friendly and indicates 'and literally so'. Aficionados will explain to you that some clues are more *&littish* than others and there is certainly more charm in those with not a 'wasted' word, but any clue where the definition and wordplay bleed into each other has a distinct appeal:

Some hitman in Japan? (5)

It would be unusual getting nays with me (3, 3)

It forms oval cone after energy's spent (7)

Stomach of shorthorn ready to be eaten? (5)

*cont'd*

Its pies are demolished (10)

For starters, romantics want a bottle of fizz here? (5, 3, 3)

Derived from one that hid a king? (5)

Royal at one time – aren't I spoilt! (5, 10)

Punctuation mark perhaps too freely used (10)

Lines portraying 'down plight' needless bullying's brought about (4, 4, 4, 6, 2, 3, 4)

# Events

*When puzzles embrace the news*

JANUARY 2004, Butler University, Indiana:
Mathematics professor Jerry Farrell takes part in an on-line interview [SEE NOTES]. After discussing a puzzle he wrote in 1996, he shares with his interviewer a special 'telekinesis puzzle' he has since constructed. The solver begins by tossing a coin. Heads or tails?

6 NOVEMBER 1996, a newspaper kiosk in New York City:
The lead story in the newspaper is CLINTON ELECTED.

5 NOVEMBER 1996, the office of the *New York Times* puzzle editor:
The phone rings. It is a crossword solver, angry that

puzzle editor Will Shortz has been using the *Times* crossword to promote his personal political views. It rings again. Another solver is infuriated by Shortz's presumption in predicting the outcome of the 53rd presidential election. It is polling day and the votes have not yet all been cast, let alone counted. The phone continues to ring ...

EARLIER THAT MORNING, in the home of a *Times* solver: Outside, people are heading to the polling stations to cast a vote for Bob Dole, Bill Clinton (or, indeed, for Ross Perot or Ralph Nader). Inside, the solver looks at the day's puzzle in the *Times*. She fills the third row from the top with the answer to 17 across's 'Forecast' – PROGNOSTICATION – and then the third row from the bottom with MISTER PRESIDENT, which directs her to the middle row. This row has two clues, both of them unusual:

**39A. Lead story in tomorrow's newspaper (!), with 43A**

**43A. See 39A**

Forty-three across is clear from the crossing letters: ELECTED. The solver frowns. Tomorrow's newspaper will of course lead on the victory of whoever is elected, but there's no way that headline, with the name of the victor, can be an entry in today's puzzle. Surely that's not the PROGNOSTICATION?

It is. The down clues that cross with 39 across spell it out: CAT ('Black Halloween animal'), LUI ('French 101 word'), IRA ('Provider of support, for short' – Individual

Retirement Account), **YARN** ('Sewing shop purchase'), **BITS**
('Short writings'), **BOAST** ('Trumpet') and **NRA** ('Much-
debated political initials' – the National Rifle Association).
The middle row reads: **CLINTON ELECTED**. The solver picks
up the telephone.

**EARLIER THAT MORNING**, in the home of another *Times*
solver:
Another solver frowns at the grid. 'Lead story in
tomorrow's newspaper'? He fills in the squares of 39
across with help from the down clues: **BAT** ('Black Halloween animal'), **OUI** ('French 101 word'), **BRA** ('Provider
of support, for short' – brassière), **YARD** ('Sewing shop
purchase' – in America, a length of fabric), **BIOS** ('Short
writings'), **BLAST** ('Trumpet') and **ERA** ('Much-debated
political initials' – the Equal Rights Amendment). The
middle row reads: **BOB DOLE ELECTED**. The solver picks
up the telephone.

**EARLIER THAT YEAR:**
The candidates in the forthcoming election are
confirmed as Bob Dole, Bill Clinton (and Perot and
Nader). A maths teacher and occasional puzzle
constructor named Jerry Farrell asks *Times* puzzle
editor Will Shortz if he remembers the puzzle which
Farrell submitted to the *Times* in 1980. Shortz does.

1980, the offices of *Games* magazine:
*Games* editor Will Shortz receives a crossword puzzle
which has been rejected by *The New York Times*. He

thinks it is 'pretty amazing', but can't accept it, as it is beyond the deadline for the November/December issue and the puzzle needs to be published before election day on 4 November.

EARLIER THAT YEAR, the office of the *New York Times* puzzle editor:

*Times* puzzle editor Eugene T. Maleska receives a puzzle from maths teacher and occasional puzzle constructor Jerry Farrell in which the entries which intersect with 1 across are devised such that the first answer in the grid can equally validly take **CARTER** or **REAGAN**, clued as the winner of the forthcoming election. He rejects the puzzle, asking: 'What if Anderson wins?' Maleska has been in the post for three years but already has a reputation for fastidiousness and fustiness. It is unclear whether his rejection is motivated by a conviction that independent candidate John B. Anderson might break the two-party stranglehold on American politics, by a sense of loyalty to another man who uses a middle initial or by a sense that the *Times* is not in the business of provoking solvers and messing with political crystal balls … and never will be.

# INTERLUDE

Here is Jerry Farrell's telekinesis puzzle:

The solver begins by tossing a coin and writing **HEAD** or
**TAIL** as 1 across in a four-by-three grid.

**ACROSS**
1 Your coin shows a ____
5 Wagner's earth goddess
6 Word with one or green

**DOWN**
1 Half a laugh
2 Station terminus?
3 Dec follower?
4 Certain male

| 1 | 2 | 3 | 4 |
|---|---|---|---|
| 5 | | | |
| 6 | | | |

In British puzzles, the best-loved topical reference was a clue published on 11 January 2001. This time, the story is best told in chronological order, beginning three centuries earlier ...

**1685** A vicarage is built in Grantchester, Cambridgeshire.

**1887** Rupert Brooke is born.

**1910** Brooke moves to the Old Vicarage, Grantchester, which now has beehives, to work on his postgraduate thesis.

**1912** Brooke writes the poem 'The Old Vicarage Grantchester' in Café des Westens, Berlin. It ends: 'Stands the Church clock at ten to three?/And is there honey still for tea?' and becomes shorthand for nostalgic love of a decent England.

**1913** The first crossword is published in the *New York World* newspaper [SEE 3 DOWN].

**1915** Brooke dies in the Aegean; the Old Vicarage is bought by his mother, according to his wishes.

**1921** John Galbraith Graham is born.

**1924** British newspapers adopt crosswords.

**1929** The first *Guardian* crossword is published.

**1931** Mrs Brooke leaves the Old Vicarage to her son's friend, the former Liberal MP Dudley Ward. It is still in good hands.

**1940** Jeffrey Archer is born.

**1949** Graham is appointed chaplain of St Chad's College, Durham, the beginning of a clerical career that will take him to a stint as a vicar in Huntingdonshire, now part of Cambridgeshire.

**1958** Graham has his first crossword published in the *Guardian*.

**1966** Archer marries Mary Weeden.

**1969** Archer becomes the Conservative MP for Louth; his career goes on to infuriate liberal-minded readers of the *Guardian*.

**1970** The *Guardian* changes its policy on its setters from anonymity to pseudonymity; Graham chooses to appear as Araucaria, after the monkey puzzle tree, and presently creates the 'alphabetical jigsaw' format, where the grid is to be filled with twenty-six answers presented in alphabetical order.

**1976** Archer publishes the novel *Not a Penny More, Not a Penny Less*, the first of a string of potboilers.

**1979** With his recently amassed wealth, Archer becomes the new owner of the Old Vicarage, Grantchester.

**1986** Archer has sex with prostitute Monica Coghlan.

**1987** Archer takes libel action against the *Daily Star* for a story about himself and Coghlan and wins £500,000 damages. The judge comments on the 'fragrance' of his wife, suggesting that it would be at the very least surprising if her husband were to do what had been alleged.

**1992** Eyebrows are raised as Archer is made a life peer and becomes known as Lord Archer.

**1993** The Conservative Party launches its 'Back to Basics' campaign, focusing on morality and the sanctity of marriage.

**1999** Jaws drop as Archer is selected as the Conservative candidate for the inaugural London mayoral election.

**2000** Archer is charged with fabricating evidence during the 1987 libel trial and expelled from the Conservative Party; he leaves politics and is left to contemplate his crimes at home. Araucaria looks for an anagram of **THE OLD VICARAGE GRANTCHESTER** using Scrabble tiles; having found 'Lord Archer', he then sees 'chaste' – 'and I knew immediately that "chaste" and "Lord Archer" could make something interesting'.

**11 January 2001** The *Guardian* publishes an Araucaria puzzle with the clue 'Poetical scene with surprisingly chaste Lord Archer vegetating (3, 3, 8, 12)'. The definition is 'Poetical scene' and the anagram of 'chaste Lord Archer vegetating' is indicated with the perfect indicator for the context: 'surprisingly'. *Guardian* solvers find four decades of pent-up spleen and indignation regarding Archer expressed with wit and economy in an ingenious and memorable eight-word rebuke.

**19 July 2001** Archer is found guilty of perjury and perverting the course of justice during the 1987 libel trial and is sent to Belmarsh prison.

**2005** Araucaria is awarded the MBE for services to the newspaper industry.

**2006** Serial killer Dennis Nilsen writes his prison diaries and announces: 'My narratives record the events of a life spent subject to maximum security conditions and is no shallow Jeffrey Archer confection.'

# Twelve months

Regular events are – well, you could say – regular
events in crosswords, where a clue may indicate the day
on which it is published. While topical references are
possible, they are also dangerous, since the news may
change between setting and publication. Moreover,
many solvers are at the puzzle page specifically to avoid
the cold, hard facts in the rest of the paper. A frisson
of nowness is still offered in the crossword, though,
by seasonal events. That way, a puzzle can remind
you what day it is, even if you want to avoid what's
happening that day.

**JANUARY:**
Vessels, any number, in bay for time of celebration
(5, 5)

**FEBRUARY:**
Devour the last of eggs, say – cooked now (6, 7)

**MARCH:**
(down clue): Traditional feast of Wagner's work
gets us up into its sequel (9, 6)

**APRIL:**
Time for silliness, unusually old as a folly (3, 5, 3)

*cont'd*

**MAY:**

Call for help when workers celebrate (6)

**JUNE:**

Time for new-age celebrations that can make customers smile (6, 8)

**JULY:**

Elegant hearty seen round about here? (6, 7)

**AUGUST:**

Festival mass held by priests (6)

**SEPTEMBER:**

Quixote – unusual man – sadly sacking you and me one day in September? (8, 7)

**OCTOBER:**

Permit drug to be used in female celebration (9)

**NOVEMBER:**

Good French spirit – almost time for today's ritual (7, 5)

**DECEMBER:**

My early hangover could come from this revelry (8)

# Vale?

*What will the crossword of tomorrow look like?*

In Chapter 3 down and elsewhere, we have declared that the first crossword was printed on 21 December 1913 in the *New York World* newspaper. Arthur Wynne's 'Word-Cross' was the rudimentary, grid-plus-clues, definitions-lead-to-answers puzzle from which all others – Swedish and Japanese, straight and cryptic – have developed.

But is that definitely, indubitably, true? The years following the American Civil War saw a flourishing of periodicals for veterans, keeping alive the camaraderie of the Union and Confederacy groupings, sprinkling in some reportage ... and the odd puzzle.

*The Neighbor's Home Mail* described itself as the 'most intensely interesting Soldier paper published in this or any other country'. Also part-temperance journal, the *Mail* urged former Union soldiers to subscribe in order to preserve 'the little incidents and precious memories which fill the bosom of every honored veteran', adding, 'Every Soldier should write jokes for it!'

In the edition for October 1874, the section of puzzles headed ENIGMATICAL PROPOSITIONS contained this challenge:

> 11. *Crossword.*—My first is in morn, but not in night; Second in wrong, but not in right; Third in over, but not in beneath; Fourth in long, but not in brief; Fifth in iron, but not in lead: Sixth in tongue but not in head; Seventh in running, but not in fleet; Whole, in awaking, we all gladly greet.  BEN E. DICTION.
>
> 12. *Drop Letter Puzzle.*—Th- w-rd -s - l-mp -nt- m- f-t -nd l-ght -nt- m p-th.  LITTLE ONE.
>
> 13. *Enigma.*—I am composed of 20 letters. My 1, 6, 3, 14, 7, is to quarrel; 10, 18, 12, is a metal; 16, 4, 8, 13, is used in guns; 5, 2, 19, 20, part of a fork; 15, 11, 9, a coin (not money,) 17 a consonant.  CAP I. TAL.
>
> ☞ Who will be the first to report the solution of all the above puzzles?  Who?

Is this crossword a crossword? Well, yes and no. Surely, goes the case for 'yes', a puzzle called a crossword which asks the solver to manipulate interlocking words is a crossword puzzle. But, counters the case for 'no', where is the grid? Ah, remarks the 'yes', but Arthur Wynne's grid is so different to those we see today. It was a diamond rather than a square, and had a strange system of numbering the clues, proving that a crossword can look quite unlike today's puzzles and still count as a crossword ...

To answer this question is not merely to split hairs; it helps us understand what the future of the crossword might be.

The chief current method of distributing a puzzle is to squish a bunch of trees until they become thin sheets of paper, then spray them with ink derived from soy juice in the shape of a grid and clues and surround them with all manner of investigations, opinions and illegally obtained voicemails. Good luck persuading the entrepreneurs on *Dragons' Den* of the sustainability of that business model.

In 1874 periodicals crammed the maximum content into the paper available, setting the type small and close together, and the nineteenth-century solver completed the puzzles on a separate sheet or in his or her head. By 1913, there was more space and more scope for diagrams, pictures ... and grids. (In 1913, too, the sight of things being chopped up and whacked back together was quite the vogue, from Duchamp's bicycle-wheel-on-a-stool to Picasso's guitar-in-pieces.) The *Neighbor's Home Mail* 'crossword' and Wynne's diamond each took a form appropriate to the workable technology of the day. As the lead blocks of hot metal gave way to digital type, the number of possible grids expanded. Crosswords have shifted with technology, and they're about to do so again.

We can understand the crossword in its current form as a result not just of the brains of the pioneering setters [SEE 17 DOWN] but also of the possibilities of First World War-era printing.

As such, the crossword comes with a set of loose assumptions which are entirely dependent on its physical form. If a crossword comes into your consciousness by means of a newspaper, it means that certain things are expected of you, the solver:

// You will need to furnish yourself with extra kit i.e. pencil or pen.

// Said crossword will be two-dimensional.

// You will be expected to complete or abandon said crossword on the day of its publication, in order to make 'room' for the next one.

// You need not by default time the solve; the setter cannot directly invite solvers to go into competition with each other.

// The setter must use the printed word, always in black, as the basis for clues and answers.

None of these, in terms of crossword pleasure, is a shortcoming, but they all begin to seem a little arbitrary when you consider what's happened to the medium the puzzle originated in. The decline in broadsheet print readership is not going away: in 2012, one paper experienced a 16.3% drop in circulation; another a 16.8% fall.

There's nothing about a newspaper's content that demands physical form – except perhaps the crossword in its current form: the final reason for newsprint to be printed. In news-rooms and editors' offices, crosswords are considered important for loyalty and news-stand sales. This is largely based on anecdote and hunch, so I decided to commission some research to see what the numbers look like.

Three days of surveying later and I was peering at a

spreadsheet which told me that, in 2013, around three in

ten British adults attempt a crossword at least once a week. Of those who solve at all (72%), just over one in five says that their choice of newspaper has been influenced by its crossword. So it looks to me like our country has 14.7 million people solving at least weekly – and 7.3 million making paper-buying decisions based at least in part on the crossword culture of the paper: the tone of the puzzles and the personalities of the setters.

The good news for newsprint is that two thirds of solvers have never attempted a crossword in any form other than on paper, in the paper; the bad news for editors is that setters might now feel emboldened to ask for a long-overdue pay rise. However, even if, on the upside, we interpret these figures as suggesting that the on/in-paper crossword is helping to hold Fleet Street together until it slides into its inevitably digital future, the crossword in its centenary year is nonetheless treading water rather than powering forwards in a butterfly. Crossworders, both setters and solvers, might benefit from their puzzle of choice switching to another paper medium, or ponder how the experience of a puzzle with the same grid and clues might change its form in different mediums: newsprint, online (on screen or printed out) and apps for smartphones and tablets.

On paper, the crossword is a physical activity, albeit not one that is likely to make practitioners break into a sweat. For some, the pleasure is tactile and being able to write the letters of an anagram on the shorts of a football player loitering on a nearby sports page is part of the process.

Orlando – a staggeringly prolific setter who has been supplying puzzles to the *Guardian*, *Financial Times* and *Times* since 1975 – created a crossword site in the early days of the World Wide Web; and in 2012 he reflected that online solvers seem to prefer to see onscreen something very like what they see on paper. 'There's no demand for the bells and whistles,' he noted – those potential bells and whistles including 'hyperlinks, sound, pictures, video, and so on'.

For those solvers accustomed by school to completing exercises by making marks on paper, who knows, there may remain in the future a vestigial two-dimensional form of the crossword. If the experience of home printing ever becomes less horrific than it is now, he or she may be printing off a daily puzzle rather than buying it from a newsagent, surrounded by all that other bumf.

One vision of this future comes from the London technology company Berg Cloud, which has produced a small home printer which automatically and inklessly produces, each morning and on thermal paper, something that is a little like a newspaper, but not quite. Users choose from features such as news, to-do lists and puzzles for consumption on the bus or train, for example: the available items include sudokus and a super-quick version of the *Times* crossword which contains two clues (super-quick, that is, assuming that they are the right two clues for your mood on a given weekday).

After the initial set-up of the Berg Cloud printer, the puzzles are simply there, every day, just like they are in the newspapers. Indeed, the past propagation of puzzles is explained in part by their presence in a paper. The crossword might not be your destination when you buy a paper – and, typically, it doesn't have anything to do with news – but a sufficiently long journey or a day with sufficiently grim reports might divert you to the crossword page: the only part of a paper which offers instant interactivity. The potential new solver is buying a crossword without realizing that he or she is doing so. But as newspapers become sprawling websites, some with a separate price package for the puzzles, the cost of entry rises.

Even for the seasoned and paid-up solver, the digital crossword is in danger of getting lost. On a smartphone or tablet, every other format of entertainment and communication is converging to jostle for the limited attention of the user of a single device – and most of the other 'gaming' options are germane to their form, asking to be swiped, tilted, stroked and tapped in new and gratifying ways: the touchscreen equivalents of Orlando's 'bells and whistles'.

Such things are not alien to the crossword: as early as 1982 the American cryptic evangelist Henry Hook, whose career was described in *The New Yorker* as 'one long effort to subvert our safe assumptions about puzzles, to make them as unsettling and unpredictable as art', showcased another approach. It was a puzzle called 'Sound Thinking', in which many of the clues were announced over a loudspeaker: his contribution to the 1982 US Open Crossword Puzzle Championship, and a perfect ten of context plus content.

The challenge for crossword setters and editors is to make wordplay work in the devices that are replacing print. New types of clue, using non-verbal hints, seem certain to emerge: some may become part of the standard armoury; some will branch off to make new kinds of puzzles, using colours, sounds and shapes, which might or might not be called 'crosswords'.

So far, most of the features publishers have added to crosswords have been along the same lines as those which adorn news: shareability, and other social accessories such as leader boards for the speediest solvers [SEE 5 DOWN]. But crosswords are not like news; they're not made up of facts but are abstract edifices in which words are spelled out in unconventional directions [SEE 22 DOWN]. Those directions currently number two: across and down – but more are possible.

One possible direction of travel is suggested by another look at the *Neighbor's Home Mail* and the puzzle in its twentieth-century incarnation. The 1874 'crossword' could be re-presented as a straight line of cells into which the solver writes the word MORNING: essentially a single across entry. For newsprint crosswords, the 'grid' metaphor (derived from a griddle [SEE 3 DOWN]) expands the area of play to a plane. Now screens can take their users in more than two dimensions and metaphors other than a grid or a plane may explode into view while the crossword remains recognizable as a crossword.

The setter Eric Westbrook is a teacher; he is also registered blind. For him, there is nothing inevitable about limiting the directions of clues to across and down, and he has quietly shown an amazing way of subtly rethinking the crossword.

When Westbrook constructs a puzzle, the analogy he uses is a block of flats. Each square becomes a room and the words may be spelled out in front of you, to your right, or down through the storeys beneath your feet. While the crossword is more engrossing, solving it does not, as you might suspect, take a lot of getting used to: the solver soon forgets that there's anything out of the ordinary going on and engages with the clues and entries.

As Eric points out, most solvers could walk through their own homes blindfolded. 'I walk around three-dimensional grids until I know them inside out and all the letters are in their places. It's not quick – but it's certainly easier than doing a school timetable.' Overleaf is a partially filled grid in which, if you adjust your eyes to reading in different directions, you can see the answers starting from square one, **CHARING** operating as an across, **CHALK** as a regular down (now going away from the solver) and **CROSS** reading (down) down.

Currently, Eric's puzzles exist in a two-dimensional medium. Having filled his grids, he recruits the UK's broadsheet setters to set the clues and prints the puzzles as calendars to raise money for the Royal National Institute of Blind People's Pears Centre in Coventry, and for Children In Need. He is certainly a maverick, but that doesn't mean he's completely out on his own: there are others, too, building in a third dimension. The *Listener* puzzle series [SEE 10 ACROSS] may be printed on the flat pages of the *Times* newspaper but it has asked its solvers

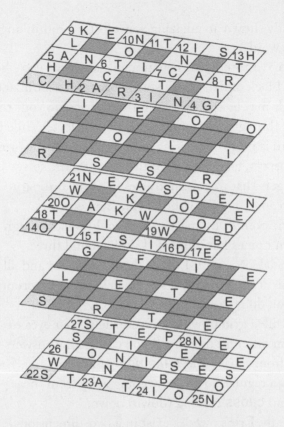

to cut out its grids and restructure them in the form of a Rubik's Cube, the one-sided loop known as a Möbius strip and even the abstract single-surfaced Klein bottle. If any puzzle embraces time as the fourth dimension – a grid in which the right letters depend on what day it is, say – it will surely be the *Listener*.

Another exciting new direction was suggested by Tracy Gray in a *New York Times* puzzle based on the 'right turn on red' traffic instruction. In its down clues, if the solver encountered the letters **RED**, he or she changed direction, so, for example, **IN SHREDS, CLAIRE DANES** and **CHEERED ON** become:

```
I                C                C

N                L                H

S                A                E

H                I                E

REDS        REDANES        REDON
```

Deviating from across and down does not mean that these crosswords are not crosswords. It merely suggests that, just as words can currently inhabit spaces above and below each other, the puzzles of the future may place them in front of and behind each other. Which is not really so big a change, is it?

# Pen or pencil?

*What your choice of writing implement says about you:*

**Pen:** You prefer deductive reasoning. You expect ambiguity to resolve itself and to remain resolved. You know that each entry in the grid is waiting for one and only one word and you withhold judgement until you are sure which one word that is. Then you can look at the crossing answers safe in the knowledge that the letters entered are correct. For you, the basic unit of information in a puzzle is The Clue. You may come unstuck, however, when The Clue might equally suggest two answers, and only the crossing letters reveal which is The Entry.

**Pencil:** You are one for inductive reasoning. You accept that even when something appears to be the case, you may have overlooked some key piece of information. You build your interpretation of the world and of a grid tentatively. You demand as much information as possible before you commit. For you, the most important unit of information in a puzzle is The Grid, and each answer depends on more than its clue. You may come unstuck when the space for a tricky clue is filled with lightly scrawled letters, some correct and some incorrect.

**Wax crayon:** You are desperate to solve, travelling with no writing implements other than something of your child's (now fourteen) which you have inexplicably found in a pocket. You will come unstuck when the crayon becomes so blunt that each letter fills four squares at once.

# 17

# Split

*The unflattering portrayal of crosswords*
*in* Brief Encounter

Noël Coward based his screenplay for *Brief Encounter* on his one-act play *Still Life*. In the stage version, housewife Laura Jesson considers an extramarital affair with charming physician Alec Harvey and all the action takes place in the refreshment room of Milford Junction railway station.

The screen adaptation shows us Laura's home life. Crucially, her husband, Fred, is not portrayed as a monster; neither is Dr Harvey a baddie. No, Fred is a kind and decent man: the villain in *Brief Encounter* is a crossword.

Consider the first time we see the married couple together. Fred invites Laura to sit by the fire and help him with the *Times* crossword; she replies that he has the most peculiar ideas of relaxation.

'Fred,' mutters the viewer, 'can't you see that your wife is forcing that smile? The last thing she wants is to listen to you calling out clues.' Yet, in the very next scene, he asks Laura to complete the Keats line 'When I behold upon the night-starred face, huge cloudy symbols of a high ...'

With an effort, Laura gives the answer, **ROMANCE**, and suggests that Fred check it in the *Oxford Book of English Verse* – he doesn't: he's satisfied because it fits with the entries **DELIRIUM** and **BALUCHISTAN**.

'Romance!' barks the viewer. 'Romance, Fred, you damned fool! Not the word "romance"; not the seven-letter string R-O-M-A-N-C-E: it's the real thing your wife is crying out for!'

Here the film declares that crosswords are a retreat from the world and from feeling – an abstraction perhaps not dangerous in itself but to be feared in that it ultimately sends respectable wives into the arms of strangers in railway refreshment rooms.

'And is it any wonder?' yells the viewer, now distraught. 'I'll tell you who *wouldn't* spend time with Laura working

out which words fit with **BALUCHISTAN**. Dr Alec Harvey, that's who. The Dr Alec Harvey who's been making her faint, that's who. Out-of-season rowing in the botanical gardens is Alec's idea of fun, being stranded in the water, helpless with laughter – not filling a monotone grid with the names of Pakistani provinces.'

And it gets worse. One evening Laura blurts out that she had lunch earlier with a strange man, and that he took her to the movies. Concentrating on his puzzle, Fred replies 'Good for you,' and goes back to pondering who said 'My Kingdom for a horse.'

Such is the grip of the puzzle on Fred's mind that he moves on to his next clue rather than addressing the reality of his marriage crumbling in front of him. Just as *Scarface* had cocaine and *Trainspotting* had heroin, so *Brief Encounter* shows the harrowing effects of crossword addiction.

'For God's sake, Fred!' the viewer is by now howling. 'Put down that newspaper and hold her in your arms!'

Happily, in the closing scene, he does. It is only as the picture ends that we see the villain – this scourge of respectable middle-class marriage, this divisive word game – vanquished. Laura's anguish is so intense that Fred, finally, lets go of his copy of the *Times*, places it beside him on the sofa and tells her: 'You've been a long way away,' adding, unbearably: 'Thank you for coming back to me.'

What gives *Brief Encounter* its power is not what is said, but what is not said: Fred's declaration – unspoken, but no less unsentimental for that – that he is giving up the evil of crosswords. That his very English repression prevents him from saying this outright makes the denouement all the more moving.

# Crosswords in cinema

Wine roadtrip *Sideways*, in which Miles Raymond
solves – in pen – two real-word puzzles set by
Alan Arbesfeld and Craig Kasper. His drink-
driving pales into insignificance against a spot of
what might be termed solve-driving.

The Coen brothers' *The Hudsucker Proxy*, in which
Amy, the Pulitzer-winning journalist played by
Jennifer Jason Leigh, hears her paper's setter
ask, 'What's a six-letter word for a condition of
the hypothalamus?' and instantly replies **GOITER**
(although it should be noted that goitres affect
the thyroid – or at least British ones do).

Cop spoof *Hot Fuzz*, in which a policeman and a
hotelier get away with calling each other a 'fascist'
and a 'hag' by 'innocently' solving the clues in a
crossword.

François Truffaut's *Le Dernier Métro*, where the
fascism of occupied France has infiltrated the
crossword: the answer to *'Un être puant'* ('A
stinking creature') is **YOUTRE** ('Yid'); and that to
*'Celui dont on ne se méfie jamais assez?'* ('Who do
we not mistrust enough?') is **JUIF** (Jew).

# 18

# Wing

*Class and politics in the daily puzzle*

Right-leaning papers tend not to bother too much with politics in their crosswords. The *Times* puzzle has a convention that no living person – other than the Queen – should be clued, which rather tends to keep current affairs out of the grid. Likewise, the *Telegraph* cryptic typically has a healthy air of detachment regarding the news that surrounds it.

Although many setters create puzzles for different papers, they mould their puzzles to fit the ethos of each publication. The papers that are most open to topical references in their puzzles are the *Guardian* and the *Independent*, which means that when politics does surface in a daily puzzle, it's more often with a tone that reflects

the philosophies of those publications. Here are three
clues by Sarah Hayes, who sets as Arachne for the
*Guardian* and Anarche for the *Independent*:

**Leading Italian politician having regular orgies and
about to be put in jail (8)**

**Tory in Lab disguise? (4,5)**

**We'd no self-worth, working here? (4,2,3,5)**

The existence of a lively leftie puzzle scene might surprise
some. During the Cold War, we were told that the Soviet
Union banned crosswords for being bourgeois and
decadent (and pioneering Russian setter Vladimir
Nabokov did not please the authorities with his early clue
'what the Bolsheviks will do': DISAPPEAR). Certainly, the
mid-century crossword had a reputation for being, if not
conservative, at least conformist: just think of the
pinstriped businessman solving on his commute [SEE 9
ACROSS]. And in the earliest days of the puzzle, Dorothy L
Sayers' toff detective Lord Peter Wimsey insisted that
solving crosswords was a perfect fit with the Tory ethos.

The story 'The Fascinating Problem of Uncle Meleager's
Will' begins with Lord Peter flouncing around in silk
pyjamas, his every step 'a conscious act of enjoyment',
helping his butler with a clue. The plot concerns a young
woman who has begun experimenting with socialism. Her
late uncle had been of the firm conviction that a 'woman
who pretends to be serious is wasting her time and
spoiling her appearance' and Lord Peter resolves to teach
this young woman a lesson by favouring her in his will but
obscuring the contents of the document in crossword

form. As she learns to enjoy the whimsical pleasures of puzzling, so she sees the wisdom of forgetting her silly ideas about social justice and begins to concentrate on less muddle-headed matters, such as marriage and getting her hair 'properly shingled at Bresil's'.

While some see wordplay itself as inherently subversive [SEE 15 DOWN], for Wimsey, crosswords are conservative because solving is an acceptance of the pleasures offered by life as it is, in contrast to all that dour campaigning for reform. Had he known that the *Times* setter Alec Douglas-Home was to become a Conservative prime minister (and had he been a real person), he could have used the fact to bolster his case.

> Once [Douglas-Home] was sitting next to someone on a train who was struggling with a crossword he had compiled. The man asked for help, and was deeply impressed when his companion got all the answers, apparently without a moment's thought.

Those pleasures are not universal, though. There are few institutions as conservative as Fleet Street and the arrival of crosswords was regarded with horror by the press of Wimsey's era: the lower orders, the papers reported with appalled disapproval, were wasting valuable working hours on solving puzzles [SEE 26 ACROSS].

Working-class solving became a national issue one morning at the Clydeside Scott Lithgow shipyard in 1981. Two welders were tackling the *Financial Times* crossword while they waited for a welding rod to be repaired; a manager told them to put away the puzzle and, when they refused, both were suspended. Following a disciplinary

hearing during which they apologized, one was further
suspended and the other sacked, and their fellow
shipbuilders downed tools.

This local incident was reported in the national press
with more than a note of incredulity. Welders tackling a
cryptic crossword? And in the *Financial Times*, at that? In
the 1980s the perception of a class divide was still very
strong: quick crosswords in tabloids were for the workers;
cryptics were for those who had had a classical education.
And there was once some truth in this division, in
crossword terms, at least: earlier cryptics contained
many clues that were not really cryptic at all but relied
instead on the solver filling the gaps in quotations
recalled from prep school; typically, Shakespeare, Keats
and the *Odes* of Horace.

So for its first half-century the crossword was divided
far more by the class of its solvers than by the politics of
its setters. But, as the broadsheets' puzzles developed into
a form which relied solely on wordplay, the distinction
began to make less and less sense. Familiarity with
literature and the sometimes highfalutin' language it
contains may be a product as much of your social
background as of the height of your brow. Wordplay, by
contrast, is open to all – exemplified by the image of Ian
Dury's aitch-dropping chauffeur father in the song 'My
Old Man' solving the *Standard* crossword as he waits at
the airport to pick up passengers.

It's all just letters. A hidden answer, where the grid
entry is concealed in the words of the clue [SEE 12

ACROSS], is there for all to see. And anyone, no matter which school's tie they wore, can stare at an anagram, jumbling its letters until it yields its secret. You might even call it the democratization of the crossword; I'd call it the cryptic finally finding its feet.

# Crosswords in the Commons

'We had half the Cabinet ministers writing to the *Times*,' recalled that paper's first setter, Adrian Bell, about the early days of its crossword. 'It made you wonder what they did in their Cabinet meetings, to tell you the truth.'

Never mind the Cabinet: Parliament itself has been sporadically disrupted when one member has caught another surreptitiously solving instead of attending to matters of state. During the seventeenth sitting of the debate on the 1980 Transport Bill, John Prescott pointedly asked Kenneth Clarke for clarification on the wording of the bill 'if he finishes the crossword in time'.

Clarke responds by reading out a putative clue – 'Four down is "undoubtedly muddled", which appropriately describes the Hon. gentleman's speech' – before being reminded by the committee's chairman that 'newspapers are not normally accepted in the House.' Advantage Prescott – except for a suggestion from the Conservatives' Roger Moate that Prescott himself

*cont'd*

would be better employed doing a crossword: 'Then he might have something to think about while he spoke.'

A newspaper need not even be present in the Commons for its crossword to create a diversion. In 2006 the Shadow Leader of the House, David Heath, sardonically congratulated the former Home Secretary Jack Straw on 'the signal distinction of being the answer to 10 across' in the previous day's crossword.

Heath added: 'The clue, however, was "Foreign Secretary no longer clutches at it", which may be a description of his performance.' Politicians can take some pleasure in the feeling that they are well-known enough to be part of a crossword clue, but in the case of **STRAW** it may just be that your name lends itself to wordplay.

# Deceit

*What counts as cheating?*

> 'I could stop drinking tomorrow.'
> 'But you won't.'
> 'No, I won't. And I won't stop smoking either, or swearing, or cheating at crosswords.'
> 'You cheat at crosswords?'
> 'Doesn't everybody?'
> — Ian Rankin's *Set in Darkness*

Inspector John Rebus is wholly unrepentant, but there's a sliding scale from sinlessness to sinfulness when it comes to filling a grid. The purest solve involves nothing more than the newspaper, a pen or pencil, and a solitary solver. It's one-on-one combat, unarmed. No reference books, no phone-a-friend and *certainly* no Internet. Anything that deviates in the merest morsel from this monastic model is, for some, cheating.

Outside of competitive solving [SEE 5 DOWN], crosswords aren't issued with terms of engagement. There're no Marquess of Queensberry rules for wordplay. By definition, you can't cheat when there are no rules, but most solvers have a sense – perhaps not articulated but running deep within them – of what is Acceptable and what is Unacceptable when they sit down and peer at 1 across.

These boundaries of fair play vary, as do the settings in  which solvers solve. Some approach puzzles in pairs, as is their right [SEE 21 ACROSS] and, even if you're going it alone, you may or may not choose to make judicious calls on those around you. In the *Friends* episode 'The One with the Dirty Girl', Rachel announces that she really wants to finish a crossword entirely by herself but is later heard suggesting to Chandler a trip to see a musical – specifically, and suspiciously, the 1996 Tony Award winner. She adds innocently that she is sure it must be good and casually asks if Chandler happens to know its name. (Spoiler alert: Rachel eventually completes the puzzle.)

That kind of moral mission-drift is familiar and can take place in the course of a single puzzle. If you were to respond to the very first clue you looked at by pulling *Roget's Thesaurus* from the bookshelf, an onlooker would be entirely justified in asking what exactly the point of the

exercise was and whether you had the slightest grasp of
what the pleasure of the puzzle is supposed to be.

When it comes to the endgame, by contrast, you might
be looking at a grid with a dusting of unfilled squares
and a couple of clues that stubbornly refuse to budge.
Then it's decision time. If you've set yourself, explicitly or
otherwise, the challenge of completing the puzzle using
your brain alone, then you must gather your strength and
return to rereading every word of the clue, coaxing new
interpretations from each, again and again and again.

But then again – again – nobody has imposed those
boundaries on you, and you may prefer to isolate what you
think is the definition and use an external source to find
some synonyms, finish the exercise and get on with the rest
of your life, or get off the bus before you miss your stop.

The rules may change over a lifetime of solving, too. An
experienced solver expects most of the action to take
place in his or her head. For a beginner, it's game on by
any means necessary. Yes, the setter is aiming to lose
gracefully and intends you to decrypt every clue; yes, you
have been given two chances in each clue, the definition
and the wordplay. But that doesn't mean that the
crossword should simply crumble before the novice. There
has to be a degree of bloodshed.

To tackle a cryptic crossword is to enjoy the experience
of your brain working in a way that everyday life rarely
calls for. You learn in perhaps hard-won increments how
to chop language into pieces and reconstruct it in the
squares of the grid. Until recently, the best way for
beginners to understand the clues that defeated them was

to buy the following day's edition of the paper and look at the answers; today, the paper's website may offer a cheat button for individual clues or the whole solution on the day of publication.

It may be educative, but the key thing is not to say, 'Ah yes, **TAURUS**, that fits,' but instead to look at the clue as well – perhaps 'He's been removed from dictionary, the beast' – and work it out: 'so we're removing the "hes" from "thesaurus" and **TAURUS** is the beast.' This is not just about the moment of revelation: it is about the future of your solving soul. As each device becomes clearer to you, your pleasure in future puzzles will multiply. If you remain baffled, most crosswords have dedicated blogs where other solvers parse each answer, so enlightenment is never that far away.

The real moral challenge, however, is certain weekend prize puzzles [SEE 10 ACROSS] – the type with bars instead of black squares and answers that include tricksy variant spellings of words used once in a poem by Edmund Spenser, or terms of abuse heard only in one of the Perths (Tayside or Western Australia). All the rules are hastily thrown out of the window; in fact, you'd be a right **COOF** (a term of abuse heard only in one of the Perths) to sit down without *Chambers* before tackling one of these.

With normal crosswords, *Collins* or the *Concise Oxford* are the reference works typically used by the setters – they have fewer obscure words than *Chambers* and better reflect the vocabulary a solver might be expected to possess. So if the setter uses those publications, does that mean it's okay for the solver to use them? Well, it depends who you ask.

Some see the looking-up of words as laudable and a sign

that the solver is increasing his or her wordpower – after all, newspapers give dictionaries as prizes for solving, and they can hardly expect solvers not to use them. Others regard a trip to the reference shelves as a sign of the coming apocalypse – and they took that view even when dictionaries were all made of paper and required a little donkey work to obtain the answer.

Nowadays, the nearest dictionary might be online or on a smartphone, in which case it may offer help of a kind way beyond the powers of a traditional reference work. With the bound, paper variety of dictionary, you need at least to be able to guess how a word begins in order to look it up and see if it's right; a digital source that allows you to use 'wildcards' lets you type in ?H?R?A?A? and confirms in seconds that you are a **CHARLATAN**.

But are you? Your sense of what is and is not fair is a declaration of self: of how you prefer to reach goals and what you like to do with your own mind. As the former *New York Times* puzzle editor Will Weng used to say: It's your puzzle. Solve it any way you want.

There is, however – of course – one crucial exception. If you discuss a prize puzzle for which the solution has not been published on an online message board or blog, you have sinned – and you know it. Prize puzzles are more than challenges of wordplay; they are communities. Entering a *Listener* puzzle [SEE 10 ACROSS] for marking is a social act; during your solve, you know that others might be asking a friend or manipulating a dictionary, but if anyone is grindingly exploiting the hive mind of the Web, that's several orders of magnitude different.

# Beyond cheating

John Gielgud wrote to *Times* crossword editor John
Grant in 1993 to say that his puzzle addiction began
in 1944, inspired by an electrician at the Haymarket
Theatre: 'I have found the crossword a sovereign
therapy during endless hours of waiting while filming
and doing television.'

His approach to filling the grid, however, was not
always sovereign. Fellow actor David Dodimead once
noticed that Gielgud was 'skipping through the clues,
neatly filling them in at an amazing pace'.

Was there nothing the great man couldn't do?
Dodimead scanned Gielgud's grid and found his eye
drawn to one entry in particular. 'Excuse me, John,' he
asked, 'what are **DIDDYBUMS**?'

'No idea,' replied Gielgud. 'But it does fit awfully well.'

# Dialogue

*How solving brings people together*

In the 2009 romcom *All About Steve* the audience learns quickly that Sandra Bullock's awkward lead character is socially maladjusted through the giveaway details of her a) being a constructor of puzzles and b) – the clincher – believing that crosswords are 'better than life'. Her best friend is a hamster. That says it all: some writers of fiction can have a tendency to use 'crossworder' as shorthand for 'oddball' or a 'loner'.

In real life the image of the solitary solver just doesn't hold up. Consider this: cryptic crosswords are not published with a how-to manual. Instruction books are available [SEE 12 ACROSS], but when you're tackling your first puzzle, it's unlikely you'll be in a bookshop and instantly drawn to buy one. There's a good chance, though, that you may not be alone.

Crosswording is most often learned from another person, under the guidance of someone who happens to be around: it's intimate, collaborative and fun. This is the best way to get to grips with the conventions and quirks of solving: engage somebody you trust to dispel the fog of intimidation.

Take the setters of crosswords. When they are asked how they got into puzzles, more often than not the answer goes along the lines of: watching mother or father (or both) solving, from afar; being invited to help with the odd anagram; superseding the parent and becoming the family's super-solver; and going on to make some sort of a living out of it. Without the last two steps, it's a similar story for many solvers.

Crosswords bind families: for example, the rhythmic exchange of texts between geographically distant siblings that accompanies their regular appointment with a Saturday prize puzzle, or the extended clan attempting a group-solve of a Christmas jumbo over those post-Christmas Day days of the holiday.

The crossword fits well in any environment in which, like Christmas, people find themselves in the same space for longish periods with little to do. New York Yankees pitcher Mike Mussina solves solo from October to March but says that puzzles are for him really a ball-season thing:

> Sometimes we'll sit down as a group and try to plow
> through it as fast as we can. Whoever's doing the

writing doesn't even get to look at the clues. They're writing so fast because of the people leaning over their shoulder firing out answers.

And you can double this for actors, whose working life involves more waiting around than actual acting. Prunella Scales met her future husband Timothy West backstage, over the course of what she calls 'a Polo-mints and *Times*-crossword flirtation', and they are far from the only couple to have been brought together by puzzles.

In 2007 Emily Cox and Henry Rathvon, the married couple who set for the *Boston Globe*, were approached by solver Aric Egmont. He had got to know his girlfriend, Jennie Bass, over the course of weekly Sunday solving sessions in a local café. This had begun on their fourth date and, for Aric, it was proof that the couple did not need a big event to enjoy each other's company: it was 'a first tiny step towards normalcy'. He asked whether a forthcoming *Globe* puzzle might contain some hidden messages [SEE 4 DOWN] meant for Jennie.

Cox and Rathvon were feeling in romantic mood – and there is surely no more exacting test of a marriage than co-setting – and the puzzle appeared on 23 September. They took care to include themed entries that would not appear too odd to most solvers but which would have a special meaning for Jennie Bass.

That day in the local café Jennie was tickled to find in the grid her boyfriend's surname, and the names of her best friend and sister, but considered it a coincidence until the clue 'Macramé artist's proposal' (LET'S TIE THE KNOT).

This was just a hint of what was to come. One hundred and eleven across was 'Generic proposal' and, as they wrote in the answer (**WILL YOU MARRY ME**), Alec went down on one knee. 'There was no reason for me to suspect it,' recalled Jennie. 'Then he got up and came back with a box, and it was pure elation.'

That answer was **YES**. Pay attention, the team behind *All About Steve*: *that*'s a romcom.

## *Desert Island* crosswords

Once you've learned to solve with a loved one, crosswords can provide solace in solitary moments – or so suggests the frequency with which they appear as books and luxuries on Radio 4's *Desert Island Discs*.

Dancer **Lionel Blair** supplemented the Bible and Shakespeare with 'a book of crosswords'; footballer **Trevor Brooking** chose the same but remembered to ask for a pencil. Bandleader **Roy Fox** asked for 'the easiest crossword puzzles I could find'. And John Gielgud [SEE 19 ACROSS] asked for Proust or a book of crosswords.

Soprano **Birgit Nilsson** had more specific puzzling requirements – her luxury item was a collection of Swedish crosswords; while *Schindler's Ark* author **Thomas Keneally** went as far as specifying the paper – 'it would have to be a collection of *Times* crosswords' – and said that he would ration himself to one puzzle each morning.

Actor **Simon Russell Beale** was the most precise of all the solvers among the castaways in his puzzle request. 'Can I have a daily crossword flown in? Not flown in – pigeoned in? Actually, there's a particular setter who anybody who does crosswords will know is the master. Araucaria. So if I could have a daily Araucaria.' Offered a pen, he said he would be happy to solve with a twig.

# Thriller

*When puzzles are used in espionage – or seem to be*

In his retirement, Meredith Gardner solved the cryptic in the (London) *Times* every day. In his working life, too, he had a talent for finding a word or phrase hidden in a mass of surrounding text. Handy for a US Army codebreaker deciphering messages from a KGB clerk who was thought to be receiving information about the American nuclear programme during the Cold War.

A KGB codebook, abandoned in Finland and partially burned, helped Gardner decipher Soviet intelligence reports, and when, in 1946, one contained the name of the leading scientists in the Western project to develop an atomic bomb, the hunt was on for informants at the Los Alamos weapons plant. Gardner deduced that there was a spy among the staff, whose wife had a name which was encoded as three characters. These three characters,

decrypted, were E—L. He twigged that the missing letter
might not actually be a letter but a word that had been
assigned its own character because it was frequently used
in English. And one of the most frequently used words in
English – well, it's been used seven times already in this
paragraph, so that would do it: 'the'.

And so in 1951 began the controversial trial for
espionage of Julius Rosenberg and his wife E-THE-L.
Their subsequent execution attracted international
concern, especially because it was not clear to what extent
Ethel had really been involved, and America was charged
by its liberal critics with nuclear hysteria. Ethel's death in
the electric chair was regretted by Gardner; Jean-Paul
Sartre went further, describing it as 'a legal lynching'.
Gardner's widow said that her husband's take was that
'those people at least believed in what they were doing.'
Putting aside the ethics of geopolitics, one lesson is clear:
don't work in the world of spying if your name can be
rendered as a cryptic clue, and especially if it contains any
of the most common English words. Andys, Theos and
Willys – your number's up.

Crosswords and modern Western intelligence agencies
came on to the scene in the years just before the First
World War; in the Second World War spycraft and
puzzles cemented their relationship.

On 3 December 1941 the *Daily Telegraph* published an
unusual letter from a Mr W. A. J. Gavin, purportedly
writing as the chairman of the Eccentric Club. A sum of

money had been enclosed with the original letter and the following challenge was issued:

> If [one of your readers] succeeds in [solving the puzzle] you are authorized to send the enclosed £100 Bank of England note to the Eccentric Club Minesweepers' Fund.
>
> My challenge, which allows 12 minutes for a solution, extends to all of your correspondents who claim to do your puzzles in such incredibly short periods of time.

The editor invited any solvers to come to the *Telegraph*'s Fleet Street offices on a Saturday afternoon. Twelve minutes was an ask, but not impossible – and 'Mr Gavin' never thought it was. The puzzle was solved, the banknote dispatched to the Minesweepers' Fund and a few weeks later twenty-five of the successful solvers who had turned up on that Saturday afternoon received letters asking them to report to a Colonel Nichols of military intelligence, 'who would very much like to see you on a matter of national importance'. One of them, Stanley Sedgewick, related what happened when he turned up:

> I was told, though not so primitively, that chaps with twisted brains like mine might be suitable for a particular type of work as a contribution to the war effort. Thus it was that I reported to 'the Spy School' at 1, Albany Road, Bedford.

The 'particular type of work' was codebreaking at the new decryption centre in Bletchley Park.

And while you would now expect codebreaking
recruitment to involve experts in computing, there was no
programmable electronic digital machine for anyone with
that kind of mind to work on. Not, that is, until Bletchley
developed just such a device: the Colossus, a loom-like
behemoth which was devoted to cryptanalysis of high-
level German army communications. Yet, powerful though
it was, the human brain was invaluable in peering at
encoded messages and spotting the most likely
substitutions of words and letter-pairs that could wring
some sense back into them.

The human decrypters had a certain temperament:
meticulousness, the ability to balance ambiguities until
they resolved themselves, patience – and a cool head. An
unnamed codecracker remembered the necessity of not
buckling under pressure:

> Just imagine the codework in front of you is a
> crossword. If you had someone breathing down your
> neck saying, 'You've got to get it done in five minutes,' it
> wouldn't help at all.

The confluence of crosswords, computers and cryptography
makes for a good argument if you ever need to defend the
hours you devote to puzzles. 'Sure, it may *seem* like an
abstract waste of time,' you can say, 'but if it was the 1940s,
I'd actually be training myself to help prevent the jackboot
of Nazi oppression from enslaving all of Europe. Could
you just excuse me a moment while I work on this tricky
anagram? Oh, and by the way, do you know what the secret
German plan to negotiate a surrender in northern Italy

was called?' By the time the other person has looked up that codename and discovered it was *Kreuzworträtsel* – Operation Crossword – and how arbitrary the name was, you'll have won the argument – or at least had enough uninterrupted time to crack that tricky anagram.

As well as playing their part in codebreaking heroism, however, crosswords have also been suspected of having been used in the service of treason.

MI5 had its suspicions when on 17 August 1942 the word DIEPPE appeared as an answer in the *Telegraph* puzzle and two days later there was a calamitous raid on the Channel port. The intelligence officer Lord Tweedsmuir, son of spy novelist John Buchan, conducted 'an immediate and exhaustive inquiry' and concluded that 'it was just a remarkable coincidence – a complete fluke.'

A one-off could be overlooked, even in a context as close to 1940s military intelligence as the crossword. But not an eight-off.

On 22 May 1944 another *Telegraph* puzzle by the same setter contained the clue 'Red Indian on the Missouri', which yielded the answer OMAHA. The Nebraskan city was not to be subject to an Allied raid, but 'Omaha' was the secret codename for the beach in Normandy where US troops were to land in a fortnight's time. This would have seemed like just another fluke – if it weren't for the fact that codenames for other D-Day beaches – JUNO, GOLD, UTAH and SWORD – had all appeared in the *Telegraph* puzzle in the previous months.

In the week and a half following OMAHA, *Telegraph* puzzles included the clues 'This bush is a centre of nursery revolutions' (**MULBERRY**, the codename for the operation's

floating harbours), 'Britannia and he hold to the same
thing' (**NEPTUNE**, the naval-assault stage) and '– but some
bigwig like this has stolen some of it at times' (**OVERLORD**,
the name for D-Day itself).

The setter, Leonard Dawe, received a visit from a pair of
MI5 agents at his Leatherhead home. Since a copy of the
Overlord plan had recently blown out of a window of
military HQ at Norfolk House, MI5 was at that point
extremely sensitive to leaks. 'They turned me inside out,'
remembered Dawe, and made him burn the notebooks he
used to work on clues, but they found no evidence that the
crosswords were being used to convey information to the
enemy.

Dawe was a headmaster as well as a setter, and in 1984
one of his former pupils, Ronald French, spoke to the
*Telegraph*. French was fourteen during the D-Day
landings and said that he and the other schoolboys used to
help fill the empty grids and that Dawe would later clue
the words they had chosen. Why, though, did that grid-
filling include secret military codewords? Because, insisted
French, the names of the operations were well known
around the school: the pupils had overheard chatter
among Canadian and American soldiers posted nearby
and picked up on the odd exciting and mysterious word.

Perhaps. The lives of agents – and suspected agents –
are, in their ambiguities, more like clues than answers,
and the schoolboy-chatter explanation is a little too neat
and decidedly too cute. Sometime *Telegraph* crossword
editor Val Gilbert suspects that someone will, when

clearing out an attic, find something that yields more details. 'I hope,' she wrote, 'they will contact the *Daily Telegraph* when they do.'

Whatever the truth, Dawe's puzzles raised serious concerns. The War Office banned the appearance of crosswords in papers headed for the Dominions (Canada, Australia, and so on) to stem a possible security breach and, following the liberation of Paris, newspapers were forbidden to publish crosswords.

MI5 was still alert to the possibility of perfidious puzzles in 1966. One Saturday in October, the *Times* puzzle had GAOL at 4 down, clued as 'This provides the stop in a sentence.' It also had RUNAGATE, a synonym for 'runaway', and ARTILLERY at 27 across. The following Monday, double agent George Blake ran away from Wormwood Scrubs gaol to a car waiting in nearby Artillery Lane. This time, it was *Times* setter Adrian Bell [SEE 17 DOWN] who received a visit from the spooks – but this time, the investigation seemed to go no further than a quiet word. Perhaps the MI5 of the sixties was more tolerant of cosmic coincidence; more likely, the technology of espionage had developed to the point where the idea of using an old-fashioned puzzle to commit treason was at best quaint and at worst ridiculous.

# Crosswords in spy fiction

As in fact, so in fiction. Espionage novels tend to use crosswords not as an element of tradecraft but as an elegiac allusion to times past. Steven DeSole, the CIA veteran in Robert Ludlum's *The Bourne Ultimatum*, considers the bygone days when spying involved archive custodians and wistfully imagines that he will answer his grandson's questions about what he did as a spy with the answer: 'Actually, in my last years, a great many crossword puzzles, young man.'

Crosswords as dotage – another common association. In John le Carré's Karla trilogy, George Smiley's redoubtable colleague Connie Sachs has been dismissed and has moved to Oxford, where 'her only recreation was the *Times* crossword and she was running at a comfortable two bottles a day.' Smiley visits her in *Tinker Tailor Soldier Spy* and sees that day's puzzle 'inked in laboured letters'.

There were, notes Smiley, no blanks. Paraphrase: her brain is still sharp, but of no use to the service. Nothing sadder than a sad old spy. The saddest thought of all, though, comes in Stephen Fry's *The Liar*, when

*cont'd*

Professor Donald Trefusis recalls his colleagues at Bletchley Park:

> It soon became clear, however, that the Enigma encryption device that German Naval Intelligence was using would need mathematicians to crack it. Acquaintanceship with the decryption techniques of the last war, the ability to do the *Times* crossword while shaving and a mastery of Russian verbs of motion were not enough any more.

On this account, the finest hour of crosswords in intelligence was also its last. Unless, of course, Trefusis was protesting too much …

# 26

# Courts

*When crosswords were considered*
*a menace to society*

> Scarcely recovered from the form of temporary
> madness that made so many people pay enormous
> prices for mah jong sets, about the same persons now
> are committing the same sinful waste in the utterly
> futile finding of words the letters of which will fit
> into a prearranged pattern, more or less complex.
>
> — 'Topics of the Times', *The New York Times*,
> 17 November 1924

The first crossword in a British publication appeared
quietly in February 1922, in *Pearson's* magazine. More
appeared over the next few years, but these were in books,
not newspapers. It was not just that the papers were slow

to see the puzzle's appeal; they were actively hostile to the very notion of the crossword.

They warned nervous citizens of the damage this scourge was doing to American citizens: Simon & Schuster's crossword books had instigated a full-blown craze across the Pond [SEE 3 DOWN]. In December 1924 an editorial in the *Times* had the chilling headline 'An Enslaved America'. The crossword, it explained, 'has grown from the pastime of a few ingenious idlers into a national institution: a menace because it is making devastating inroads on the working hours of every rank of society':

> Everywhere, at any hour of the day, people can be seen quite shamelessly poring over the checker-board diagrams, cudgelling their brains for a four-letter word meaning 'molten rock' or a six-letter word meaning 'idler,' or what not: in trains and trams, or omnibuses, in subways, in private offices and counting-rooms, in factories and homes, and even – although as yet rarely – with hymnals for camouflage, in church.

The choice of 'idler' as an example of a clue is not, I suspect, an idle one. As with video games and recreational drugs, crosswords alarmed the self-appointed defenders of morality because people who are solving a crossword are simply enjoying themselves. Five million man-hours, warned the *Times'* New York correspondent, are being lost every day as workers forget their duty to contribute to gross national product, lost in the pure pleasure of finding synonyms.

And because of this, the *Tamworth Herald* reported in the same year, pernicious puzzles 'have been known to break up homes'. This family-wrecking comes about when husbands spend time solving a clue rather than earning a crust. The solution of one concerned policeman was to enforce on addicts a ration of three puzzles a day, with ten days' imprisonment if a fourth was attempted.

In February 1925 the *Times* announced that crosswords have, with 'the speed of a meteorological depression', crossed the Atlantic. 'The nation still stands before the blast,' the paper thunders, 'and no man can say it will stand erect again.' Prepare yourself for some mayhem.

'The damage caused to dictionaries in the library at Wimbledon by people doing cross-word puzzles,' we read later that year, 'has been so great that the committee has withdrawn all the volumes.' In Willesden, it's the same sad story. Dulwich Library, meanwhile, starts blacking out the white squares of crossword grids 'with a heavy pencil,

to prevent any one person from keeping a newspaper for more than a reasonable length of time'.

Those selfish paper-hogging solvers! Meanwhile, booksellers bemoaned falling sales of the novel – no longer itself considered a menace to society – in favour of 'dictionaries, glossaries, dictionaries of synonyms, &c'. The *Nottingham Evening Post* went on:

The picture theatres are also complaining that crosswords keep people at home. They get immersed in a problem and forget all about Gloria Swanson, Lillian Gish, and the other stars of the film constellation.

And it gets worse. In another part of Nottingham – poor, puzzle-blighted Nottingham – the zookeeper is swamped in correspondence. The reason? Crosswords, of course.

Correspondents [are] unabashed over requests for aid in solving 'cross-word' puzzles, and the Zoo at least will be relieved when a new hobby takes the place of the current one. What is a word of three letters meaning a female swan? What is a female kangaroo, or a fragile creature in six letters ending in **TO**?

Across town at the theatre, the stage is bare:

Mr. Matheson Lang ... missed his entrance in the Inquisition scene through becoming absorbed in a puzzle. This caused him much chagrin, for he is extremely conscientious as regards his stage work.

Who is safe from this funk? Surely the world of grocery is unblighted? Sadly not:

A girl asked a busy grocer to name the different brands of flour he kept. When he had done so, expecting a sale, she said she didn't want to buy any. She just thought one of the names might fit into a cross-word puzzle she was doing.

Worrying stuff. Happily for society at large, the crossword was soon to find itself pursued by the law. Prizes had

started appearing for puzzles – another symptom of the
something-for-nothing culture, tutted the *Times* – along
with a new variant on the crossword that would seem very
unfamiliar to the solver of today.

It is said that 'the street finds its own uses for things',
and the same is true when the Street is Fleet. By the end
of 1926 the *News of the World*, the *People*, the *Daily Sketch*
and the *Sunday Graphic* were among the papers to print
prize crosswords which were not only 'pay-to-play' but
had multiple clues for which there was more than one
correct answer. The grids contained far more black squares
than normal grids – the reason for which became clear
when you reached a clue such as 'You look forward to
getting this when you are in hospital.' Solvers who hoped
that their choice between **BETTER** and **LETTER** would be
decided by a B or an L in another clue found that there
was no such other clue. The crucial squares stood alone. If
you did manage to complete the grid correctly, a prize was
offered – but those ambiguities ensured that the number
of 'correct' entries for each puzzle would be tiny.

The immense popularity of these puzzles made them
very lucrative for the syndicates and newspapers that
created them, and court summons were issued by the
police, who insisted that they were not crosswords at all
but thinly disguised lotteries. A lawyer for the police
argued at Bow Street that 'the words are ridiculously easy,
and a child of 12 should have no difficulty in solving them.'
At times it seemed that the crossword itself was on trial:
thanks to the Betting and Lotteries Bill, it became literally
as well as morally criminal.

However, the genuine crossword benefited in invidious comparison: as the judges shut down the lotteries, the puzzle survived. Indeed, the crossword was on the way to becoming respectable. The *Telegraph* had started publishing one on 30 July 1925 and, by the end of the decade, the *Times* had started to wonder if these puzzles were so bad after all. Or, in the words of BBC correspondent Martin Bell, whose father was the *Times'* first setter, the paper 'was losing circulation hand-over-fist to the *Telegraph* because the *Telegraph* had the new-fangled American fashion, the crossword, so the *Times* had to get one pretty sharpish'.

The motivation might have been financial and the volte-face a tad hypocritical after all the scaremongering, but the appearance on 1 February 1930 of a puzzle in the paper taken by 'Top People' marked the crossword's move to unambiguous respectability. Soon the *Spectator* and the *Listener* followed and Fleet Street began to rely on puzzles for a good, and indisputable, proportion of its news-stand sales, as some readers would buy a copy, have a bash at the crossword then throw the paper away unread.

# Taking the biscuit

The puzzle mania of the twenties expressed itself in many forms: for example, black-and-white designs began to appear on earrings, dresses, collar pins and cigars.

The most opulent manifestation of the craze was a Broadway revue, *Puzzles of 1925*, which featured a scene in a Crossword Puzzle Sanatorium filled with those driven to madness by puzzle fever.

And the most audacious was surely the product launched in 1925 with the announcement: '"Eating our own words" is a familiar phrase. Eating crosswords is a new pastime, but a pleasant one since Messrs. Huntley and Palmers, Ltd. have put on the market their "Cross-word" Cream Biscuit.' The competition puzzle which helped to publicize the snack is on display in the University of Reading; sadly, none of the original biscuits remain.

# 27

# Unamerican

*English, the best crosswording language*

Like many American inventions, the crossword became, in the twentieth century, a global phenomenon. Browse at newspaper kiosks and bookshops around the world, and you'll see Greek, Persian, Japanese and Tamil surrounding those familiar-looking grids. However, the crossword is not ubiquitous – some languages do not take kindly to being broken into pieces and plotted in interlocking squares.

Where it does appear, the culture of crosswords adapts to its environment. Some differences are visual: in South American puzzles, the clues live in the grid, printed in tiny type with arrows indicating the direction of the answer; and the squares of the smaller Japanese grids each take one syllable rather than one letter.

More important – and something for its speakers to

celebrate – is the greater scope afforded to setters who
work in English. English may be called a Germanic
language, but it's more like a *mélange, salmagundi* or
*omnium-gatherum*: for any English word with a German
origin, there may well be a perfectly useable alternative
brought to Britain by the Norman French, or something
with a Latin flavour. And so, as Oxford Dictionaries
carefully word it, 'it seems quite probable that English has
more words than most comparable world languages.' So
there are many different ways of denoting the same objects
and actions, but all are valid parts of the English lexicon. If
you want to hint at some word or other, you don't have to
start with a dictionary-style definition. No wonder the
English language is well suited to the crossword.

*Times* editor George Geoffrey Dawson wondered if
there were any better reason for the existence of words
such as **CADI, EFFENDI, MUEZZIN** and **VIZIER** than 'to get
crossword composers out of trouble'. It's as if Dawson had
tried to construct a puzzle himself, got frustrated when he
found he'd set himself into a corner which needed a very
unEnglish-looking word and then realized that some
exotic term imported from Turkey might just do the job.

It's certainly true that English has always been happy
to absorb words from places with which Britain has traded
or which have been part of its empire, thus further
expanding the vocabulary available to the creators of word
games. In the case of quick crosswords, the existence of
different words with the same meaning means that more
clues can be written using pleasing short synonyms rather
than tedious descriptions such as 'African city'. The surfeit

of English words also means that puzzles only occasionally need to use the names of people and places, which are staples of many non-English crosswords.

The existence of multiple words for any one given thing makes English not especially friendly towards non-native speakers trying to learn the language, but on the upside, it's perfect for games that involve words, terms, designations, expressions and utterances.

The obverse is also true: the existence of so many words with multiple meanings is a boon to setters. Want to write a cryptic clue where a perfectly ordinary word turns out to signify something quite different? English is your language. Better still, it is spoken in Britain, a country where it's possible – and some believe integral to the national character – to get away with not quite meaning what you appear to be saying. Yashmeen Halfcourt, in Thomas Pynchon's *Against the Day*, may overstate the case for that uniquely British ironic distance when she insists that 'all English, spoken or written, is looked down on as no more than strings of text cleverly encrypted' – and she cites crosswords as evidence – but her version of Britain, where 'no one ever speaks plainly,' is a good fit with this country's crosswording culture. This is the humour of the cryptic clue, which might not mean what it says, but certainly says what it means [SEE 1 DOWN]. As the crossword devotee Sandy Balfour put it:

> It is such a British idea: that you can say one thing and mean another, and yet have said what you meant. It's a

brilliant, brilliant notion and of course it's played out time and time again in crossword puzzles.

Wordplay aside, there are two visible manifestations of the Britishness of British crosswords. One is the grid. Since the solver is given two routes to the answer in a typical cryptic clue, he or she needs less help from the letters provided by those answers which cross with it – and so fewer do cross with one another, leaving the grid peppered with more of those black squares. A crossword that's largely white is one where the setter is confident that, even if you lack the vocabulary for a specific entry, if you answer all those that cross with it, you'll have filled it in without even trying. In British cryptics, more onus is placed on each individual clue to suggest an answer.

The other difference is the presence of the setter's name. A cryptic clue is an expression of the personality of the setter who wrote it – and the same goes for the inventive, playful definitions found in such American puzzles as those in *Newsday* and *The New York Times*. In non-English-language puzzles, named setters are rare and the crossword sits on the puzzle page, impersonal and apparently aloof. Why put your name to a list of synonyms? English-language setters, having all those extra words to play with, are, in contrast, regarded more like authors. And rightly so.

# How do you translate a crossword?

In Georges Perec's French-language novel *La Vie mode d'Emploi*, we find an unfinished puzzle in the room of one of the characters reproduced in the text. The rest of the book is riddled with cross-references, puns and hidden expressions, so the task facing the translator is daunting: how do you recreate a collection of words, preserving not only their meaning but also the characteristics which allow them to intersect with each other in a grid? And, since a seasoned solver might look at the grid and wonder which words might fit the empty spaces, should the gaps be taken into consideration too?

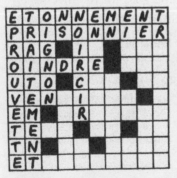

Happily, Perec was aware of this potential problem and furnished his German translator Eugen Helmlé with notes about the novel's wordplay. In the case of the crossword, his instructions were that only **ETONNEMENT** and **OIGNON** mattered. And so, in David Bellos's English translation, we see **ASTONISHED** and **ONION** among other unrelated words. Bellos told me that the inclusion

of a potential **TLON** in his version of this fictional puzzle
is a nod to the imaginary world in the title of Jorge
Luis Borges' 'Tlön, Uqbar, Orbis Tertius', which seems a
suitably *perécienne* flourish.

```
A S T O N I S H E D
P O ■ N       ■
A L   I
R I S O T T O
T L   N   ■
M O
E O
N U
T Y ■
S S N O R M A N D Y
```

He added a regret about
his translation of the grid:
the placement of **ONION**
means that there's an
impossible entry ending
with O in the English
version of the grid. So if
you have a copy of *Life: A
User's Manual* you should
pull out a pencil and add an extra black square to the
grid, in the space immediately following **ONION**.

And if you're an experimental novelist with, for whatever
reason, a grudge against translators, you might consider
creating a book featuring a puzzle in which the clues,
the entries and the way they intersect is vital to the plot.
A translation of the clues would be likely to necessitate
a different grid, and vice versa. As Bellos remarked, 'It
would be a paradoxical and fuse-blowing project.'

# 28

# Ibex

*Words found more often in grids than in real life*

> 'I should think that 90 per cent of the people believe
> that there was but one Roman emperor, and that
> his name was Nero.'
>
> — Prime Minister Stanley Baldwin
> to a Press Club luncheon

Crossword English is a twisted version of the language. Do enough puzzles and you'll soon become more familiar with the Italian river the **PO** and the Sumerian city-state **UR** than you would ever otherwise have been, and you'll start to think of sailors as **TARS**, even though it's no longer the eighteenth century.

Such words occur more regularly in crosswords than they do in, say, conversation. Some are good at making up parts of other, longer expressions; others fit conveniently into a grid when you need, say, a four-letter word with a vowel at each end, like ASEA: made entirely of very common English-language letters.

Most solvers develop a feel for such words, but Noah Veltman went one further and got some figures and lists. Through solving he had become attached to words such as OLEO and OLIO and started to take an interest in their regular appearance. He took a database of the clues and answers in the *New York Times* crossword from 1996 to 2012 and compared the frequency with which words appear there with how often they crop up in another context: Google's database of 20 million books.

One word that doesn't appear in any of those 20 million books is 'crosswordiness', Veltman's splendid term to denote a word's quality of appearing more often in a crossword than in real life – or, at least, one measure of real life.

The constellations with names beginning URSA, the Texan mission the ALAMO, the name NOEL, the spirit ARIEL, the proofreader's instruction STET and the ardent desires known as YENS are among those words that score highest. All of them, when judiciously placed in a grid, increase the number of possible words for the entries that cross with them because of the presence of vowels and other oft-seen letters, or of those letters which, like Y, are often found at the end of a word. This also explains why, as crossword setter, editor and teacher Don Manley puts it in the *Chambers Crossword Manual*, you can 'expect to find ELEMENT and EVEREST frequently, especially along the edge,' offering a bounty of those Es with which so many other words end.

Part of the job of a crossword editor is to make sure that the 'crosswordiest' words don't become tiresome – and kudos to all the editors for this ongoing fight. But don't be mistaken: shunning cliché is not the same as making crossword language the same as our everyday lexicon. Manley continues by asking the solver to forgive the setters their fillers. 'Learn to regard them,' he advises, 'as old friends.' Indeed, many solvers enjoy the discovery of new words through puzzles, and for any familiar entry there will always be a setter with a fresh way of cluing it. Georges Perec, the French setter and experimental author, describes well this ever-increasing pressure on the makers of crosswords:

> The shorter words which hold the grid together make the greatest call on the setter's ingenuity. Some words only really exist in crosswords: the famous IO, EON, LAI, ITE, ERS, ANA, IBN and BEN as well as RU, PAT, MAT, INO, ENEE and UTE; the setter makes it a point of honour to find for each of these a clue that no-one has used before.

Here's to that honour, and here are ten of the English language's most crosswordy words, the unusually shaped faithful friends to setters, and ones you meet sooner or later in Crosswordland.

ALEE: The lee side of a vessel is the one that's sheltered from the wind. ALEE can be an adverb meaning 'away from the wind' or an order to put the helm towards the lee. It goes back at least as far as the fourteenth century and, as even the most casual fan of medieval alliterative debate poetry can tell you, is to be found in the anonymous poem 'Mum and the Sothsegger'.

**ARGO**: Reimmortalized in Ray Harryhausen's stop-motion animation *Jason and the Argonauts* were the Greek heroes who sailed on the **ARGO** in search of the Golden Fleece. In American clues, the entry can also be clued as 'Cornstarch brand' after the sauce-thickener that may have cannily coined its name so as to appear near the top of alphabetical product lists.

**ASEA**: Hyphenated in the Oxford dictionary and defined as 'On the sea, at sea; to the sea', **ASEA** also lends itself to misleading definitions via the names of the various bodies of waters, such as in *New York Times* setter Bob Klahn's pert clue 'In the Black?'

**EMU**: Words that start and end with a vowel are always useful, and sometimes those vowels just have to be E and U. Alternatives do exist: **EAU** is used in English as a fancy way of saying 'water' and the European Union once experimented with the **ECU** as its single currency. But **EMU** is the go-to entry when you just have to end a three-letter word with a U. The less frequent appearance of the **EMU** in crosswords was mourned repeatedly by P. G. Wodehouse [SEE 8 ACROSS].

**ERATO:** The inspiration – if you happen to be an ancient Greek – for lyric love poetry, and far more beloved of crossword setters than her sisters **MELPOMENE,** **TERPSICHORE** or Beryl Reid's favourite [SEE 9 ACROSS], **POLYHYMNIA.** A favoured ruse of cryptic setters is to employ 'muse' as a verb rather than a noun to disguise references to this desirable five-letter string.

**IAMBI:** In the Greek whence it comes, a lampoon, because of the tradition in satirical verse of following a short beat with a long. 'The woods decay, the woods decay and fall,' wrote Tennyson in the da-dum da-dum form known as iambic pentameter. Iambus is the singular term if you're into analysing the basic units of poetic rhythm, and two or more of these 'feet' are **IAMBI.** Can also be clued rudely, as with Monk's 'Feet using which I can go either way?'

**PSST:** If you count Y as a vowel in all but name, there are vanishingly few four-consonant words. **CWMS**, the plural of a Welsh valley, doesn't really count since W is standing in as a vowel, as anyone who's passed a 'Snwcer Hall' in Cefn y Dyniewyd can testify. **TBSP, TSPS** and other terms you might find in recipe books are, of course, abbreviations hence, strictly, illegitimate, so in *Chambers*, you're left with two interjections: **BRRR** and **PSST.**

**SMEE:** The second-most crosswordy word in Noah Veltman's analysis, **SMEE** has changed its role as an answer. Once teasingly depicted in a *Punch* cartoon in which one duck tells another that she is a **SMEE**, 'only found in

crosswords', the avian type – which may also be a smew, a
pochard, a wigeon or a wagtail – has given way to the
pirate who, we are told in *Peter Pan*, 'stabbed without
offence', as in John Lampkin's *Los Angeles Times* clue
'Barrie baddie'.

**SOHO**: Hunting used to take place on the lands to the west
of London's Wardour Street, and it seems likely that the
Anglo-Norman phrase hollered by huntsmen –'Soho!'
(which *Oxford* decides is 'probably of purely exclamatory
origin') – gave the boho district of London its name.
'Hunting call originally sets off hounds' onslaught', as
Tramp deftly clued it. **SOHO** can be also rendered with a
hyphen, as in *Two Gentlemen of Verona* ('Run, boy, run,
run, and seek him out. / So-ho! so-ho!'); in the form
SoHo for the Lower Manhattan neighbourhood that's
**SO**uth of **HO**uston Street; and all in capitals for those who
work remotely in a 'Small Office Home Office'.

**STYE**: Edward Moor's 1823 *Suffolk Words and Phrases: Or,
An Attempt to Collect the Lingual Localisms of that County*
defines this word as 'a troublesome little excrescence or
pimple on the eye-lid' and prescribes the application of a
gold ring; today, the preferred treatment is a warm
compress and some painkillers.

# New chestnuts

Some forms of wordplay are so pleasing that, even though a seasoned solver has met them before, they still raise a smile. Here are five clues that breathe fresh life into familiar devices:

Sort of stall for the frisky carthorse (9)

Very worried about final courses (8)

Side order of synthetic cream (10, 4)

Vegetable popular in French tavern (9)

Achilles, or his heel? (6)

# 1

# All The Same?

*Setters may play tricks but must also play fair*

From the 1850s onwards, Lewis Carroll devised a stream of puzzles for magazines. While they were ostensibly set for children, their linguistic and mathematical demands were beyond the capabilities of many of his adult readers. Had the crossword been born a half-century earlier, it's no stretch to imagine Carroll as one of the greatest setters in the game, probably more likely appearing in the *Listener* [SEE 10 ACROSS] than in the weekday puzzles. His fictional characters show, to varying degrees, a keen grasp of what we would now call 'the setter's art'.

'Then you should say what you mean,' the March Hare went on.

'I do,' Alice hastily replied; 'at least — at least I mean what I say — that's the same thing, you know.'

'Not the same thing a bit!' said the Hatter. 'Why, you might just as well say that "I see what I eat" is the same thing as "I eat what I see"!'

Crossword setters disagree on many things [SEE 13 DOWN] but they all follow something that has become known as Afrit's Injunction, which was given in the introduction to the 1949 collection *Armchair Crosswords* by pioneering cryptic setter Prebendary A. F. Ritchie., the headmaster who took his *nom de guerre* from an Arabic demon [SEE 17 DOWN]. 'We must expect the composer to play tricks,' insists Afrit, 'but we shall insist that he play fair.' After this, in bold:

> *You need not mean what you say,*
> *but you must say what you mean.*

No decent setter wants any of the clues in a puzzle to remain unsolved, but if the solver is well and truly stumped, Afrit's Injunction means that, when you see the answer that defeated you, you should be able to look back at the clue and see that you *could* have solved it. Take this, from a selection of the all-time favourites of *Times* readers:

**Cold display unit for seafood (11)**

In this case, the setter most definitely does not mean what he or she is saying: the answer has nothing to do with a chill counter that smells of smelt: it's not a stand of fish. But the setter *has* said what he or she means: although 'cold' seems to indicate 'refrigerated' in the context of the

clue, it's also a perfectly fair synonym for **STANDOFFISH**.
As Afrit says, a cryptic clue 'may attempt to mislead by employing a form of words which can be taken in more than one way, and it is your fault if you take it the wrong way'. Point taken.

So, the Mad Hatter would make a fine creator of crosswords:

> *'The question is,' said Alice, 'whether you* can *make words mean so many different things.'*

Humpty Dumpty, on the other hand, would not:

> *'When I use a word,' Humpty Dumpty said in rather a scornful tone, 'it means just what I choose it to mean – neither more nor less.'*

# False friends

English is a language that abounds in ambiguity, and crosswording is a language that exploits this haziness. If there's one rule of thumb when attempting to cut a path through the obscurifying fog created by the setter, it's this: the more naturally a clue reads, the more the solver must doubt its bona fides. If you get tripped up by one, don't get frustrated: think of it as a kind of friendly punnishment.

*When you see*: '**number**'
*A reasonable interpretation is*: something like one,
    or even pi
*But not in this clue*: Number of people in a theatre (12)
*See also*: a letter can be a landlady, a tower a horse, a sewer
    a seamstress – and a flower is so often a river in
    crosswords that seasoned solvers get tripped up when
    the word is actually used to mean a piece of flora ...

*When you see*: '**detailed**'
*A reasonable interpretation is*: comprehensive, meticulous,
    blow-by-blow
*But not in this clue*: Iron suit detailed? (4)
*See also*: decrease (iron), delight (extinguish), defile
    (remove from the cabinet) ...

*When you see*: **'supply'**

*A reasonable interpretation is*: to furnish, equip or provide

*But not in this clue*: Supply cocaine, damn practical (3–8)

*See also*: other anagram indicators which hide their true
        purpose – rent as in torn, cuckoo as in mad, cast as in
        thrown, and many, many more …


*When you see*: **'wicked'**

*A reasonable interpretation is*: amoral, heinous or abominable

*But not in this clue*: Supporters of wicked things (12)

*See also*: other words which change sense when pronounced
        differently: minute, pate, multiply, wound, bower,
        drawer, refuse, sow, console …


*When you see*: **'Nancy'**

A reasonable interpretation is: Sinatra, Mitford,
        Pelosi or Drew

But not in this clue: Nancy's one composer to sort out (7)

See also: R(r)eading, P(p)olish, J(j)ob, A(a)ugust, S(s)lough


*When you see*: **'does'**

*A reasonable interpretation is*: I do, you do, he or she does

*But not in this clue*: It melts just above freezing – maybe does
        without it (2–4)

*See also*: words which have the sense that they appear to
        have, but figuratively: worried meaning ate, speller
        meaning witch, flight meaning stairs, worker and
        soldier meaning ant …

# 2

# Impolite

*Why solvers need to know their slang*

At Christmas 1966, the *Guardian* held a competition in which readers were invited to send in crosswords. The winner was David Moseley. He received six guineas and an invitation to submit more puzzles – which he has now, as Gordius, been doing for nearly half a century. However, amidst the praise for his winning entry, there was a caveat: 'There are one or two things that I wouldn't normally let through. "Booze" is slang and you use it twice.'

Nowadays, any crossword editor would still judge that any crossword with the same word twice is a less satisfying solve, but **BOOZE** would pass without comment. In the sixties, though, the crossword was younger and anxious to appear respectable. University slang such as DON was acceptable, but BOOZE? A little uncouth.

Soon enough, though, the puzzle was to change its tone. The crossword editors of the sixties and seventies became less keen on certain types of clue, often impenetrable to newcomers or suggesting that crosswords are only for a rarefied clique. And so disappeared from crosswords those Latin phrases and biblical quotations which had peppered the earliest puzzles. They are lamented by few: in solving terms, they are less satisfying, since either you know them or you don't; most importantly, they are closer to a general-knowledge quiz than they are to wordplay. They're certainly not cryptic.

Some other areas of language had to fill the space vacated by outcasts such as CAIN and PERSONA NON GRATA, and the wider culture was becoming less self-conscious about slang. Moving with the times – and times where it's not unusual to hear prime ministers use terms like LOL (Cameron), BLIMEY (Blair) and FRIT (Thatcher) – and with dozens of new grids appearing every day, each requiring words which meet the unpredictable criterion of fitting with the other entries, it would be rash now to try and make the case for excluding colloquialisms. Some pieces of antiquated argot persist: a royal marine is very rarely referred to as a 'jolly' nowadays, but the word's capacity to masquerade as an adjective when it really indicates RM (a more common way of saying 'royal marine') has given it legs.

With fewer literary clues and more idioms, there has been a subtle shift in the tone of crosswords – nudging away from language as the solver might find it in prose and poetry and towards the language he or she actually uses. And today's setters are lovers of language – argot is language, after all – as it is spoken as well as written. Slang and setting are a good match: the unstoppably fertile linguistic invention of the vernacular makes it utterly irresistible to those who mangle language for a living. Particular joys are multiple words which describe the same thing, and the multiple things that can be described by a single word.

Solvers would be well advised to know what words are have edged their way into *Chambers*, *Collins* or *Oxford* recently or in the past, however nefarious the activities they describe.

Present-day solvers aren't expected to be frequent users of cocaine, notwithstanding Stephen Fry's former habit, as related in a 2011 interview with Laurie Taylor, of taking the drug before tackling the hardest British crosswords. They would, though, do well to acquaint themselves with its nicknames: ICE, C, COKE, CANDY, READY-WASH, CHARLIE and BLOW, as listed in *Chambers*. And of course a setter might induce you to take a hit of a heroin synonym such as HORSE, H, JUNK, SNOW and SUGAR. Drug use is an area of criminality that has to hide what it really wants to say, so drug slang abounds in ways of not quite saying what you mean, which happens to be the meat and potatoes of crosswords. And what can beat 'drug' to indicate the most common vowel in English? You could almost suspect that ecstasy was given its shortest nickname by setters bored of using 'east' (E on a compass), 'Spain' (E on the back of a car) and 'base' (2.71828, or *e* in a mathematical formula).

Sometimes even a dictionary is not enough.

**OMNISHAMBLES**, meaning more than just a bit of a disaster, was first uttered by the fictional spin doctor Malcolm Tucker in a 2009 episode of political sitcom *The Thick of It* and started being used at real-life Westminster and in political sketches soon afterwards. By 2012, it may not have shuffled its way into any of the print dictionaries, but it had happily trundled into crosswords, for example Nimrod's clue 'Riot in Westminster? Order nuts to stop hoax, having crossed bishop'.

It certainly has the irresistibility mentioned above, and conveniently combines two senses of 'shambles' – the awfulness suggested by the shambles which is a trestle table covered in raw meat and the clumsiness of a shambling gait. Later in 2012, *Oxford* made **OMNISHAMBLES** its 'Word of the Year'; perhaps it will appear in a future edition, but it's cheering to note how crosswords got there first. It is testament to the ear for a good new phrase possessed by setters that they embrace such words before even spellcheck and online word-finding services – and it has the added advantage of stymying solvers who 'cheat' [SEE 19 ACROSS].

Be it classical allusion or contemporary slang, the basis for a word's inclusion in a crossword – that is, a setter's judgement as to whether the average solver can fairly solve a clue for it – is as good a yardstick as any for the exciting progress of a language. The same applies, *mutatis mutandis*, to the rest of the messy world of popular culture.

Crosswords, divested of a spurious respectability, now

represent and re-present the world as the setter expects the solver to find it. Where once **PRESBYTERIAN** was a remarkable anagram of 'best in prayers', it's now just as pleasing a jumble of 'Britney Spears'.

# A bad clue?

On 7 January 2012 the *New York Times* used the clue 'Wack, as in hip hop' for ILLIN. Word soon reached the national press that a solver had complained that 'wack' has a negative sense, making 'illin', in fact, its opposite. The tone of the coverage was generally derisive: how could those tweedy crossword-constructor types expect that experimenting with hip-hop terminology could result in anything other than embarrassment?

Crosswords are slightly older (when the clue was published, ninety-eight years old) than b-boying (around forty years old), but there's a good reason why puzzlers might take an active interest in hip-hop: both activities enjoy flipping the meanings of words. Hence, in crosswords, clues such as 'To show or not to show?', which exploits two meanings of SCREEN, and 'Chopstick?' for CLEAVE. In crosswords and in hip-hop, this ambiguity is quite deliberate (that's 'quite' as in 'completely', not as in 'to a limited extent').

As Run-D.M.C. helpfully pointed out in their track 'Peter Piper', the big bad wolf which can be found in your neighbourhood is not 'bad' meaning 'bad' but

*cont'd*

'bad' meaning 'good'. See also **WICKED** – though F. Scott Fitzgerald did have a character use that word in a positive sense in 1920.

And so it is with **ILL**. In 1979 the Sugarhill Gang used it in a negative sense: offering a choice between acting civilised and acting real ill. But by 1986, the Beastie Boys were boasting of being the most illin-est b-boys and in 1989 LL Cool J praised a woman whose physique was ill. If there were any doubt this is praise, 'ill' here rhymes with 'dressed to kill' and 'dollar bill.'

Which means that even if **WACK** has started to mean 'good', the clue is sound either way. That is to say, it's not bad. Before sanctioning a crossword editor for a lack of oversight, consider whether the clue really deserves a cool response. You might think better of it.

# 3

# Origin

*How the crossword first appeared in 1913 and became an overnight sensation in 1924*

Liverpool's two greatest gifts to the world of popular culture are the Beatles and Arthur Wynne.

— American setter Stanley Newman

Between 1830 and 1930, 40 million people emigrated from Europe, over 9 million of them heading from Liverpool for the New World. One of them was Arthur Wynne. The son of the editor of the *Liverpool Mercury*, Wynne spent most of his newspaper career working for the empire of print mogul William Randolph Hearst. His legacy, though, is a piece of space-filling for the *New York World*, a Democrat-supporting daily published by Hearst's rival, Joseph Pulitzer.

The *World* mixed sensation with investigation and it was Wynne's job to add puzzles to the jokes and cartoons in 'Fun', the Sunday magazine section. He had messed around with tried-and-tested formats: word searches, mazes, anagrams, rebuses. The word square was another reliable template for teasing answers out of readers, but it's very limited. Each answer appears in the grid twice: once as an across and again as a down. Very pleasing in terms of symmetry – whether foursquare square or tilted to make a diamond – but there are only so many words that fit with each other in this way.

It's also a less demanding challenge for the solver: in a four-by-four word square, say, as soon as the first four-letter word goes in, once across and once down, the grid is 44 per cent filled.

For the Christmas edition of the *New York World* on Sunday 21 December 1913, Wynne tried something new. What if the entries read differently across and down? And so, without fanfare, it appeared.

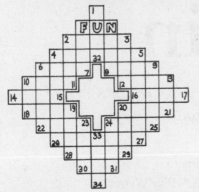

Fill in the small squares with words which agree with the following definitions.

2-3. What bargain hunters enjoy.
4-5. A written acknowledgement.
6-7. Such and nothing more.
10-11. A Bird.
14-15. Opposed to less.
18-19. What this puzzle is.
22-23. An animal of prey.
26-27. The close of a day.
28-29. To elude.
30-31. The plural of is.
8-9. To cultivate.
12-13. A bar of wood or iron.
16-17. What artists learn to do.
20-21. Fastened.
24-25. Found on the seashore.
10-18. The fiber of the gomuti palm.

6-22. What we all should be.
4-26. A day dream.
2-11. A talon.
19-28. A pigeon.
F-7. Part of your head.
23-30. A river in Russia.
1-32. To govern.
33-34. An aromatic plant.
N-8. A fist.
24-31. To agree with.
3-12. Part of a ship.
20-29. One.
5-27. Exchanging.
9-25. To sink in mud.
13-21. A boy.

Written by Wynne, it is the very first crossword. Puzzles nowadays don't come with an instruction to 'fill in the small squares' and would be more likely to clue DOH with reference to Homer Simpson than by 'Fiber of the aguti plant', but it's recognizably a crossword. Or, rather, a 'Word-Cross'. Wynne's name is just as good a way of describing the pastime as the more familiar version, but a typographical anomaly two weeks later offered the alternative 'Find the Missing Cross Words'. The following week's heading announced a 'Cross-Word Puzzle', and that's the version that stuck. It was to be some decades later that the name decisively shed its fussy capitals and sporadic hyphen.

It includes one answer twice (DOVE), and the clue for MIRED is misleading, but there it is: a new thing in the world. The most important thing about the first puzzle is that big 'FUN' across the second row. It might have been there because it was the name of the Sunday supplement, but it also served as a manifesto for crosswording. Individual puzzles may or may not be edifying, challenging or distracting, but they must always be fun. After all, nobody is forcing solvers to look at them.

agate is the name for the size of type once used by newspapers to cram as much information as possible into a small space and applied to racing results, classified ads... and crosswords

The second most important thing is the squares. Double acrostics and word squares tended to offer only the clues: the solver put the answers together in his or her head, or found somewhere to write the letters. But twentieth-century printing technology made it easier to offer a depiction of the problem that was both clearer and more enticing, the little boxes staring up from the newsprint, begging to be filled.

The first production of *Pygmalion* also took place in 1913; in the introduction to the printed version, George Bernard Shaw holds forth on the intricacies of shorthand. From wordplay such as spoonerisms [SEE 15 DOWN] to artificial languages like Esperanto and Ido, the pre-war period was one of linguistic innovation and reinvention, and rising newspaper sales and the age of mechanical reproduction helped to make the crossword the most widely disseminated way of messing around with words. Even with the reader-compiled puzzles published in the *World*, though, it remained only a weekly phenomenon, and for the first ten years of its life it existed only in that one newspaper. It had its devotees but nobody spotted its potential until the faddish twenties arrived.

It became known to millions more Americans in that decade when it started appearing outside the *World* – and

not in other papers, but in books. On 2 January 1924 the aspiring publisher Dick Simon went for supper with his Aunt Wixie, who asked him where she could get a book of Cross-Words for a niece who had become addicted to the puzzles in the *World*. Simon mentioned the query to his would-be business partner, Lincoln Schuster, and they

discovered that no such book existed.

On the one hand, this was good news: they had formed
a publishing company but so far had no manuscripts to
publish. On the other, their aspirations for Simon &
Schuster were considerably higher than a collection of
trivial puzzles. The compromise was a corporate alias
named after their telephone exchange: Plaza Publishing.

The next difficulty was where to get the puzzles? As a
first step Simon and Schuster approached the sub-editor
who had been appointed by the *World* in 1920, Margaret
Petherbridge, who, being both young and a woman, had
been assigned the suitably lowly task of fact-checking the
crosswords to try to reduce the volume of letters of
complaint, and now found her intended career in
journalism permanently on hold.

Petherbridge was offered an advance of $25 to assemble
enough puzzles for a book. Simon and Schuster decided
to attach a sharpened pencil to every copy, priced it at $1.35
and spent their remaining pre-launch money on a one-
inch advert in the *New York World*. Their campaign pushed
the idea that the crossword was The Next Big Thing :

1921 – Coué
1922 – Mah Jong
1923 – Bananas
1924 – THE CROSS WORD PUZZLE BOOK

Long-shot business ventures rarely end well – the
typical results are penury and shame. But the stories of
failure are not often told, and this is not one of them. This

is one of those familiar but wholly anomalous stories of unlikely triumph – where a bookseller friend of Simon buys twenty-five copies as a gesture of friendship but has to order thousands more; where the *World*'s top columnist, Franklin P. Adams, had predicted that Simon & Schuster would 'lose their shirts', only to start a piece four months later with the announcement: 'Hooray! Hooray! Hooray! Hooray! The Cross-Word Puzzle Book is out today.'

It is also a story where:

// Each of the four collections published that year topped the non-fiction bestseller list.

// The second edition, priced at a more modest 25 cents, received from one distributor an order for 250,000 copies – then unprecedented in the US.

// Simon & Schuster's crossword compilations became the longest continuously published book series.

It was the making of one of the major world publishers and, as rival firms produced their own puzzle series, it was excellent news for publishing in general – especially as, unlike pesky authors producing books of fiction or non, crossword setters would work for little or even no pay. The only downside for publishers was a side-effect of the fierce competition: Simon & Schuster offered to take back unsold crossword collections from bookshops, thereby instigating the practice of 'returns', very beneficial to mega-chains but increasing the element of risk for publishers ever since.

It was also the making of the crossword. The most intense interest in crosswords ever was in mid-twenties America, and was largely centred on books of puzzles. It was only later that the newspaper reclaimed its status as the default home of the crossword. However, perhaps even more important than the number of solvers solving was the way the form matured. In 1926 Margaret Petherbridge had taken the name Farrar following her marriage to John C. Farrar, founder of another publishing giant, Farrar, Straus and Giroux. As Margaret Farrar, she tidied up the messy conventions of crosswording: she may have become involved with puzzling by chance, but she thought deeply and effectively about what made one crossword better than another.

Modern-day solvers (or 'solutionists', as they were

**Apropos of Nothing**
*He:* WHAT DO YOU DO WITH YOUR OLD CROSSWORD
PUZZLE BOOKS AFTER THEY'RE ALL FILLED UP?
*She:* OH, I PUT THEM IN THE GUESSED ROOM.

sometimes described in the twenties) baffled by Wynne's system for numbering clues have Farrar to thank for the cleaner '1 across' format, and for the number in brackets that tells them the length of the entry, saving them the trouble of padding their fingers across the grid. Her preference for answers of at least three letters makes for a more satisfying experience, and the aesthetics she proposed for the grid are now characteristic of all puzzles (except for wilfully experimental exercises such as those in the *Listener* [SEE 10 ACROSS]).

Margaret Farrar's parameters for an aesthetically pleasing grid are: symmetry, a minimum letter-count of three in answers and 'all-over interlock' (the grid does not have separate sections and the solver can travel from any part of it to another).

Farrar's ingenuity was finally rewarded in 1942 when she became the *New York Times'* first crossword editor. Wynne had quietly retired in 1918 and died in Clearwater, Florida, in 1945. When the first crosswords appeared, he had wished to patent the format. Lacking the necessary funds for the process, however, he asked the *World* to contribute and was told by business manager F. D. White and assistant manager F. D. Carruthers that 'it was just one of those puzzle fads that people would get tired of within six months.' In 1925, he did, however, obtain a patent for 'an improvement or variation of the well known cross word puzzle' in which the cells formed a kind of rhombus. Sadly, for him, it never took off.

We should be very glad that Wynne failed to 'own' the crossword. Even if such a claim were enforceable, given the puzzle's obvious debt to earlier diversions [SEE 6 DOWN], it is precisely the freedom of the format and the deviations from its original structure that have made crosswords such a rich format and such a satisfying pastime. Had the crossword been patented, it would indeed have been quickly forgotten and filed under 'obsolete wordplay', between the clerihew and the cryptarithm.

# The metaphors of the crossword

A gridiron is a lattice-shaped arrangement of metal
bars useful for griddling food or torturing people
(in the very real sense, not in the way people tend
to use 'torturer' to describe a tricky setter). Its use
in the form **grid** as a metaphor to describe the
lines on maps and other diagrams seems to have
started in the First World War, which means
that when the crossword was born, 'grid' was not
available to describe its shape.

In the fourteenth century, a **clue** was a ball of thread.
Those balls are useful for finding your way
out of mazes both literal (kudos, Theseus) and
metaphorical: the Elizabethan poet Michael
Drayton bemoaned 'loosing the clew which led us
safely in', leaving him 'lost within this Labyrinth
of lust'. Later, you didn't need the maze as part
of the metaphor, and might use the word in the
context of detection: Charlotte Brontë's Caroline
Helstone announces that 'I have a clue to the
identity of one, at least, of the men who broke my
frames.'

*cont'd*

In the early days of crosswording, answers were described as **lights**, meaning clues – a confusing state of affairs, which reflects the helpful hints you get as soon as you write some letters in the grid.

Joining the gird is another instrument of torture, the cross, from which we get the sense of going side to side denoted by **across**. And if an Old English speaker needed a word which gave a sense of the direction you have to go when leaving the top of a hill, of course there was **down**.

Finally, a crypt can be an underground hiding place, or a vault in a church – or, if you're the subject of religious persecution, both simultaneously. Francis Bacon used **cryptic** as a noun to describe communication using secret methods; Agatha Christie used it as an adjective when the meaning of some words or behaviour is not immediately apparent.

# 4

# Nina

*When puzzles contain more than just
the answers to the clues*

In 1945 a daughter was born to the American caricaturist
Al Hirschfeld. She was named Nina. From that day, he
concealed the letters of his daughter's name somewhere in
most of his drawings. The letters N, I, N and A are wholly
inessential to your enjoyment of any of his cartoons, but
lie there as a treat, woven into someone's hair or the folds
of their clothing, if you know what you're looking for –
much like Alfred Hitchcock's cameos, which can be seen
in almost all of his films.

 'Ninas' is a more charming term than 'alfreds' and lives
on as a way of describing hidden extra elements that can
be discovered in completed crossword grids. They're not
part of the solve, but they raise a smile on the faces of those

who spot them. 'Nina' was first used to denote such an element by the setter Roger Phillips with reference to the definition-only *Times* 2 puzzle. While 'quick' crosswords are apparently simpler, they are often set by the same people who compile their cryptic cousins. It is easy to imagine that their constructors might prefer to set themselves a more satisfying challenge than inauspiciously assembling twenty-odd words and finding the according synonyms.

Having a hidden structure is also a good way to get started, rather than sitting there pondering the infinite possibilities of a blank grid like Buridan's ass in the fable, who finds himself stuck between two equally attractive piles of hay and, unable to rein in ambivalence and choose a favourite, dies of hunger.

There are assuredly many setters for whom the basic unit of crosswording is the clue and not the grid, and who relish each clue as it comes. For others, filling a grid may raise the unanswerable question of where to start. If you know that you're going to try and construct a grid, though, whose perimeter reads **TOBEORNOTTOBETHATISTHEQUESTION**, well, you know what to do, as you find yourself willingly thrown in at the deep end.

That's one reason for including a nina. Another is political. Take Hungary. Crosswords were banned there in 1925 when the Horthy government discovered that a monarchist setter had hidden the message **LONG LIVE OTTO** in one of them. And, when the final edition of the *News of the World* was being prepared among the debris of the phone-hacking scandal, executive Rebekah Brooks may have had two senior colleagues comb the copy for

messages from disgruntled staff, but did not notice some
seemingly pointed phrases in the clues for the quickie and
the cryptic. Set, one suspects, less in sorrow than in anger,
they included 'woman stares wildly at calamity',
'catastrophe', 'stink' and 'criminal enterprise'.

Other 'personal' ninas are happier and subtler: birthday
wishes to loved ones which, ultimately, have only one
intended reader but which are so unrelated to the
mechanics of solving the puzzle that those for whom it is
not meant would be churlish in the extreme to resent their
presence: much better to join in and relish the fun.

Among the most common ninas are when setters use a
theme in a puzzle but decide not to announce it – and you
the solver only spot that it's there if you're letting your
brain wander around. In 2009 Brendan set a puzzle for the
*Guardian* in which the answers included PIERCE ('break
through'), LINCOLN ('city'), GRANT ('admit'), HOOVER
('clean') and FORD ('go to other bank'). It is easy to miss
connections like this – especially if your obsession is the
speed of your solve [SEE 5 DOWN], but, once you do spot
them, the heart is lifted, and there are extra treats, like the
unchecked letters in the central column spelling out the
by-then-inaugurated OBAMA.

If you suspect that there's something more going on in
a puzzle than meets the eye, cast your eye around the
spaces that aren't the answers. If the grid is made up in a
Stickle-brick-like arrangement, where the outer edge
alternates white and black squares, it might be worth
reading the answers contained within them, clockwise or
anti-clockwise, to see if there's something there. The same

goes for the inner rows and columns where white cells alternate with black, and the diagonals. Spotting a nina mid-solve, perhaps in an inattentive moment, can make the endgame a lot smoother, as you may be able rapidly to fill in more squares, and hence gain more letter clues to the actual clue clues.

Ninas are also a way for setters to flex their muscles. One of the people who has done most to popularize the cryptic crossword in America is setter Henry Hook, who showed his setting chops at the age of fourteen. His grandmother gave him a puzzle which was part crossword, part jigsaw, created by Eugene T. Maleska, who went on to become the editor of the *New York Times* puzzle. Its endgame revealed a zigzagging nina reading YOU HAVE JUST FINISHED THE WORLD'S MOST REMARKABLE CROSSWORD. Days after Hook received the gift, Maleska received a puzzle, written by Hook, with the nina WHAT MAKES YOU THINK YOUR PUZZLE IS MORE REMARKABLE THAN MINE? Most ninas, it has to be said, are considerably less bombastic, but many serve a similar purpose: to prove one's chops to one's peers. They also convey an extra aspect of the personality of the more playful setters, raising spirits and making a personal connection with the solver. in a way that would surely be absent if a solver were to find a message 'hidden' inauthentically by a computerized setter programmed to so do [SEE 20 DOWN].

The paper which seems most nina-friendly (though, of course, you never know what you've missed) is the *Independent*, which goes hand in hand with its open policy regarding modern subject matter, colloquialisms and occasionally abstruse themes. In this paper, you see what happens when the nina becomes self-referential. One setter, a maths professor who creates puzzles as Monk, managed to construct a grid in which the outermost columns spelled NINA NINA NINA NINA. The playful Jambazi set a puzzle where the unchecked letters in the top row read SPOT NINA and the main diagonal began SIMONE. (Special mention should also be made of his clue 'Finally Nina Simone introduced My Baby Just Cares for Me playing classic song', which yields YESTERDAY.) The paper's most wildly nina-ish nina, though, did not mention ninas by name and is all the balder for that. The setter Phi is one from whom regular solvers have come to expect ninas, to the extent that you could spend some time scouring the

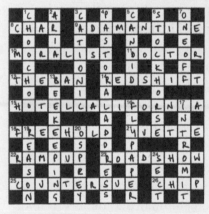

completed grid of one of his puzzles in 2012 for one of these optional-extra treats only finally to glean, inadvertently or otherwise, that there is a deeply hidden message starting in the third square of two down[SEE GRID ON LEFT].

At the other end of the scale is the *Times*, which eschews all jiggery-pokery in favour of solid, consistent cluing. Even the *Thunderer* makes the odd exception, though. There might be something hiding on Christmas Day, say, or the day of a royal wedding, or for an anniversary of the puzzle itself.

One column in the thousandth *Times* Jumbo in September 2012 read **JUMBO CROSSWORD JUBILEE**, and a row of letters which did not cross with the down clues spelled out **FOR THE 1000TH**. And cryptic crossword number 25,000 contained a trick not merely in the grid but, in addition, in acrostic form among the clues, the first letters of which read **THE TWENTY-FIVE-THOUSANDTH CROSSWORD**.

This restraint makes it all the more affecting on the rare occasions that the paper has an 'unofficial' nina. In 1967, a teacher at Westcliff High School for Boys wrote to the *Times* to ask whether a clue might be included on the day of departure of Alfred Bately, the head of maths and an ardent *Times* solver. But then, in a letter to a fellow teacher, came the curt response 'that the crossword was certainly not the place for passing on personal messages!'

That seemed to be the end of it, until the last day of the same term. Hidden in that day's apparently staid and anonymous puzzle were references including **MATHEMATICS, GOODBYE MR CHIPS** and even **ALF**. 'It rapidly became clear to us,' said a colleague (Mr Hart, John) in a letter to the *Times*, 'that the crossword editor was not as stony-hearted as his letter had led us to believe.'

Just as touching is the story of Wing Commander Peter Flippant, who entered the 1999 *Times* Crossword Championship. Having been eliminated at the first round, he offered his help as a companion-in-arms with the arrangements, in his words, 'moving chairs and tables around and shuffling pieces of paper'.

A couple of months later, the Saturday *Times* puzzle contained, with zero fanfare, the following laudation in

answers placed consecutively in the grid: **SQUADRON**
**LEADER, PETER, FLIPPANT, THANKS.**

The nina in its purest form, though, is probably the
perimeter message of a *Financial Times* puzzle by Monk.
It reads **AGHBURZUMISHIKRIMPATUL**, which is exactly the
kind of gobbledygook that suggests that the solver has
embarked on a wild-goose chase: after all,
**AGHBURZUMISHIKRIMPATUL** means nothing, even in a
made-up language, surely?

Not so. It means something in the made-up language
Black Speech, invented by J. R. R. Tolkien for the
inhabitants of Mordor. In fact, it is inscribed on the
golden, inaccessible One Ring in the *Lord of the Rings*
trilogy:

> Ash nazg durbatulûk, ash nazg gimbatul,
> Ash nazg thrakatulûk agh burzum-ishi krimpatul.

And so our nina perimeter does mean something – 'and
in the darkness bind them' – monumentally irrelevant to
the working of the puzzle as a crossword but a source of
jaw-dropping joy and hats-off admiration to a tiny
proportion of solvers. The nina, then, in a nutshell.

# Home oaf owns

The *Telegraph* Quick Crossword habitually engages in hidden wordplay: the first two, three or more across entries, when spoken, turn out to sound like something else. Here are twenty sometimes eye-watering examples, all of them proper nouns:

| | |
|---|---|
| SURE LORE COMBS | PEAK ASS SOW |
| MARS HELP ROOST | EVIL INN WAR |
| CHATTER NOUGAT | ROCKS EMU SIC |
| WHIT NEW STUN | BILK LYNN TUN |
| BARELY OWES | BOOK ARREST |
| DAMN ASS CUSS | HAMMER DAIS |
| TOOTING CARMEN | SERVANT TEASE |
| TANS SUN NEAR | HOARSE TRAY LEER |
| BUST TURK EATEN | AGE HEWED |
| BASIL FALL TEA | BRUISE WILLIES |

# 5

# Swiftest

*Is there any point in timing your solve?*

> Got up
> Had shave
> Did *Times* crossword
> Had another shave

> — Roger McGough

On Saturday 19 December 1970 the *Times* published a letter in which diplomat Roy Dean mentioned that he had completed the paper's crossword in four and a half minutes. 'At six o'clock that morning,' Dean remembered, 'I was woken from a deep sleep by a call from BBC Radio 4 saying that they were sending a car to bring me up for an interview on the *Today* programme.'

In the studio, presenter Brian Redhead produced a stopwatch and that day's edition of the *Times* and asked Dean to solve it on air. Dean was surprised – and also dismayed, as the Saturday prize puzzle was then the hardest of the week, a meatier proposition than the daily he had completed in under five minutes earlier that week.

It was not long before listeners heard Redhead announce: 'I don't believe it – that was three minutes forty-five seconds!' Dean later learned that, due to an error at the printers, the Monday puzzle – then the easiest – had been substituted by happy mistake.

The signatures of the *Today* programme team were authentication enough for the *Guinness Book of Records*: Dean was listed as the fastest crossword solver and his record stands, a generation on. Nowadays, the online version of the same paper's puzzle times your solve automatically. You can of course ignore the little clock; certainly, if you nip off to answer a call or make some lunch, the numbers accumulating in your browser window don't mean much.

Some day, though, you might solve the puzzle in one sitting and feel that you did so fast-ish by your own standards – which might mean twenty minutes or might mean a couple of hours. You might even see yourself on the day's leader board. You won't be at the top, though. Accept it: however fast your solve, you won't be at the top. At the top will be a time like four minutes, and you can be fairly certain it wasn't Roy Dean who posted it. Because, another day, you'll see the top time is two minutes thirty seconds. Two and a half minutes. These timings, you will

suspect, were not verified by anyone, much less the *Today*
team. Two minutes is barely even time to write in the
answers, let alone to solve the clues that suggest them.

These 'leaders' are people, you further suspect, who have
already completed the puzzle – in the paper version, or
using another online account. Only then have they started
a timed solve, solely in order to enter the solution
mechanically and take the credit for an implausibly
impressive time. Two questions arise: why would anyone
cheat? And, more importantly, why, even if you're being
honest, would you measure the time it's taken you to solve
a crossword?

The first question is simpler. Being able to solve a
crossword is used as a shorthand for intelligence,
especially if it is done quickly and especially if it is the
*Times*. So, however bogus your technique, being listed as
the person who can do it the quickest puts you in an
exalted position.

More intriguing is the need for speed. Two more
questions, then. Why the timing, and why the *Times*? It's
partly because of that paper's erstwhile standing as the
country's journal of record, and partly because it has a
consistent setting style. Your mileage-per-hour will
inevitably vary when solving the *Independent* or the
*Guardian*, because of the appearance of themed puzzles:
if a crossword marks the centenary of Mark Twain's death
or is peppered with the discography of David Bowie, it
tests more than your 'pure' solving skills. As the author
and setter Colin Dexter [SEE 18 DOWN] put it when
discussing the difficulty of various papers' puzzles, 'the

*Times* maintains its traditional position in the upper-middle category, with the firm dedication of its setters to "fair play".'

So the *Times* is the only British paper with its own championship of speedy solving, which began in 1970, with 20,000 entering the first stage. Just like the online leader board, the times taken to solve the puzzle at this annual event are implausibly low. They're genuine all right, but for most solvers they're just as fantastic as the made-up ones.

Take serial winner Mark Goodliffe. *Times* crossword editor Richard Browne said of him: 'We give him the hardest puzzles we do and he finishes them each in eight minutes.'

If the benchmark set by Roy Dean makes those eight minutes seem leisurely, consider this: it's something like sixteen seconds for each clue, including writing in the answer. It's so staggeringly fast, it doesn't really mean anything. When you're measuring the time Mark Goodliffe takes to do a puzzle, you are simply measuring a different thing than how long the rest of the world takes when sitting down with a crossword.

There is a Swedish guitar player called Yngwie Malmsteen. His speed and precision in playing are such that the Xbox 360 game *Guitar Hero II* has a Yngwie Malmsteen Award for players who manage to play 1,000 notes correctly in succession on its replica guitar. The point of the plaudit is that Yngwie's fervent style is almost impossible to replicate – but of course this doesn't mean that there's no point anyone else ever picking up a guitar.

Mark Goodliffe is crosswording's Yngwie Malmsteen. His is a spectator sport. Truly, it's worth watching – from afar.

One pleasure for the spectator of competitive solving is seeing which words slow down the Roy Deans and the Mark Goodliffes. In 2011, for example, Goodliffe lost some valuable seconds over RAISINY, because, as he put it, 'when you come across words you don't know then it's difficult to convince yourself they're right.'

Another annual treat in the current championship is the increasingly gritted-teeth gag from perennial runner-up Peter Brooksbank. Goodliffe skipped the 2007 final because his wife had given birth two days before. Brooksbank quipped: 'If he could be persuaded to have another one, that would be useful.' A later wheeze: 'You could slip a mobile phone into his pocket and get someone to phone it.' In 2010 he was terser: 'I'm going to have to kill him.'

A gag, of course, but one that reveals the stress of competitive solving. You can see the havoc wrought by crossword competitions played out in real time in *Wordplay*, the 2006 documentary about the American Crossword Puzzle Tournament that was held in Stamford, Connecticut, until 2008, and at the New York Marriott hotel at the Brooklyn Bridge since then.

In the early sections of the movie we see non-competitive solvers – comedian Jon Stewart and former president Bill Clinton – smiling over grids and discussing the pleasures of puzzling. In invidious contrast are the faces of the time-obsessed entrants, in particular that of Al Sanders. Sanders makes it through to the final, and in fact finishes first – but after he announces 'done', he notices that he has omitted to fill in two squares. The sight of him hurling his noise-reduction headphones to the floor, then gasping, red-faced and bent double, is evidence of the inevitable result of timing crosswords.

Is it worth it? And does it hold up, the idea that the fastest solvers are the cleverest people? 'I don't know many people who can do the *Times* crossword more quickly than me,' notes Stephen Fry in his autobiography. 'There again I do know dozens and dozens of people vastly more intelligent than me for whom the simplest cryptic clue is a mystery – and one they are not in the least interested in penetrating.'

Intelligence, however defined, is at best one of many requirements for champion-speed solving. What are the others? A clue is given by Paul McCarthy in his book about competitive Scrabble, *Letterati*. In the 1970s, McCarthy writes, most Scrabble players considered the game a literary activity, 'based on natural vocabulary and education'. Since then, though, it has become apparent that you can do well at competitive Scrabble without needing any knowledge or interest in the words other than their usefulness as letter strings within the rules of the game.

Nothing wrong with memorizing word lists, it need hardly be said, but that takes us a long way from whiling away an evening by a pub fireside, enjoying the tactile exercise of toying with some wooden tiles and seeing where they take your mind. And it brings us a little closer to another kind of Scrabble player: the computer you compete with in digital versions of the game. Likewise, in crosswords, if you're serious about increasing your solving time, you'd better be prepared to start acting a little less human yourself. Memorize those lists. Train yourself in a kind of automatic writing so that you can use those scribbling seconds to start reading the next clue.

There are also sacrifices to be made. One pleasure that you have to surrender, or at least postpone, as soon as you press the stopwatch button is savouring the setter's craft. The enjoyment of solving comes not merely from completing the grid but also from each clue in itself. The surface readings are economic pieces of language that appear to do one job and reveal a quite different purpose under close examination. Buddha would not thank you for skimming a book of zen koans, though he would probably forgive you.

The best clues have been slaved over, refined and re-refined by a setter to achieve something close to perfection in imagery and structure. I know that when I've done fast solves – either because I know my bus journey is coming to an end or because I've succumbed to the lure of the stopwatch – it's my enjoyment of each of these surfaces that has suffered. It's certainly not the context in which to save until last a multi-word answer you suspect you're going to find amusing.

Crosswords provide moments of heartening self-discovery – an 'I never knew I knew that!' – as a distantly recalled fact or piece of language enters the grid. Other times, they offer a meditative remove from the world around you: an escape from your problems, or a means of clearing your head before returning to them. If you agree that these are all mental moments to be treasured, then take your time.

Solving a crossword is entering an abstract space in which the possibilities literally lead in different directions – across and down and, on multi-word answers, flying through wormholes across the grid. Once you're sufficiently convinced that such-and-such a word belongs in the grid, there's no need to hurry on to the next. Really. Try it.

Go back and reread the clue and marvel at how what is now evident had been hidden from you in plain sight. Reread the clue and recover the sense it originally imparted. Think of it as a line of verse, or the beginning of a short story. Imagine how that story would continue and who it reminds you of. Put down that crossword and call that person. Brew coffee. Leave the grid for an hour. Leave it unfinished. Unless you're solving in under, say, ten, what, really, is the difference between, say, 11, 20 or 120 minutes?

The world benefits from Slow Solving, and the movement starts here. Wouldn't it be better if online puzzles came with their timers hidden by default?

# How to speed your solve

The most legendarily fast solver was the ghost writer M. R. James. A letter to the *Times* [SEE 1 ACROSS] claimed that, before starting his day as provost of Eton, James habitually finished that paper's puzzle while cooking a soft-boiled egg. The humorist E. V. Lucas wrote that he had tried to emulate James to help speed his own solve. 'I started at 8.00,' he wrote, 'and it is now 15.05 and the egg has burst.'

If you insist on tackling crosswords faster, here are some more helpful techniques:

As you write in each answer, start reading another clue. Get used to writing while reading (and solving).

Reshape your 'E's. Will Shortz says that modifying his handwriting has saved him 'time both in solving and in life'. Restructure your handwriting around fast strokes of the pencil.

Have someone tell you a joke before you start solving. Neuroscientist Mark Beeman found that college students performed better at word-association puzzles if they had been shown a video of stand-up comedy beforehand than if they had watched something boring or scary.

*cont'd*

Wear earphones. Better still, earphones playing white noise. Finalists in the American Crossword Puzzle Tournament listen to a recording of the background noise from the lobby of the United Nations building in New York to block out all distractions.

Use a pencil and a rubber. *Times* Championship winner Peter Biddlecombe adds: 'If you think that a letter is unclear, be prepared to rub it out and write it again.' No pen.

Start in the bottom right-hand corner. Serial champ John Sykes did so, believing that the setter may have written those clues last, when less inspired.

Try to get the beginnings, not the ends of words – beginnings have more variation and yield their secrets faster.

Check. As Will Shortz said in his welcome to the 28th American Crossword Puzzle Tournament: 'If either you leave a letter out or you make a mistake, that will cost you 195 points. The champions generally spend a little extra time after they finish a puzzle, looking it over, making sure that every square is filled and that nothing silly has been put in a square.' And if you are merely timing yourself for fun, you haven't finished at all if there's a single misplaced letter. Your time is, sadly, infinity. Check again.

# 6

# Bygone

*The prehistory of wordplay*

> At Thebes, the monster gave this clue: what has a
> head but no tail, a mouth but no teeth, a bed yet
> nowhere to sleep? That seems to me the earliest
> crossword clue. And the answer was **RIVER**.
>
> — Former *Sunday Times* crossword editor Barbara Hall

The cryptic crossword is a twentieth-century concoction.
Its grid is modern, but the devices used in its clues are as
old as the practice of looking at words and finding
meanings other than those which immediately appear.

We operate most of the time on the basis that for any
word or sentence there is a single, graspable sense. But
sometimes we want to see an invisible sense, one that has

been put there by a spy, say, or a higher power – and so many of the ingredients that make up a cryptic were once associated with the magical, the divine or the supernatural.

## THE RIDDLE

When the *Guardian* setter Paul used this clue ...

> **Old poser's bit of leg captivating copper and rated sexy (6)**

... to indicate SPHINX, he chose to make the definition part ('old poser') an allusive, cryptic description of a monster which itself had a penchant for setting riddles. 'Which creature,' the sphinx demanded, 'walks on four legs in the morning, two legs in the afternoon and three legs in the evening?' Crossword equivalents are generally terser, like the *New York Times'* 'Big piece of crust?' for CONTINENT, but the intention is the same: to describe the answer while appearing to depict something completely different.

There was of course greater jeopardy when the Sphinx asked you a question: you'd be strangled if you got it wrong, rather than leaving some gaps at 13 across; even Oedipus, who got it right, received as part of his prize marriage to a woman who turned out to be his mother, so it was really a lose-lose proposition.

Outside of *The Hobbit*, the form of the riddle is nowadays most often found in child-friendly jokes – *What*

*has teeth but no mouth? A comb!* – and in the definition part
of cryptic clues.

## THE ANAGRAM

What joy it is for the setter, tester of our wits, when he or
she discovers an anagram that relates to the answer. When
*Guardian* setter Rufus uses the words 'racing tipster' to
clue the answer STARTING PRICE, the pleasure is of pure,
unexpected coincidence, since the phrases share no
etymological roots. It's hard, in fact, to accept without
question that there's nothing more to it than coincidence:
that the letters ACEGIINPRRSTT happen to be sortable into
two phrases you might see at the same place.

In the ancient world, words were more than playthings
and coincidences more than a source of amusement. If one
word could be jumbled to make another, it was thought,
there had to be a reason. Such was the thinking of many
ancient prophets, who, writes the anthropologist Marcel
Danesi, 'were essentially anagrammatists who interpreted
this heavenly form of language'. If anagrams were a means
of obtaining information sent by a higher power, then
being good at solving them made you a soothsayer. If you
could give the king a bunch of anagrams of the names of
the members of his court, he might well think you'd found
a way of revealing their innermost characters and
intentions, and your prize for being good at jumbling
letters would be gold.

So it remained for centuries. John Taylor, 'The Water-Poet', devised such flattering anagrams as I AM A TRUE STAR (Marie Stuart), MUSES TARI AT (James Stuart) and, for the countess Rachel Wriothesley, HOLY LIVER, CHAST EVER. If you're being feted in this way, it would be rude to insist on precise recipes and reply with a quibble like 'But you had to split the W into two "V"s to make that work!'

Dame Eleanor Davies, wife of seventeenth-century poet and politician Sir John Davies, insisted that she was infused with the spirit of the biblical prophet Daniel, as revealed by a near-anagram, the laudatory, adulatory REVEAL, O DANIEL. A dean in her court, however, used 'the Dame' to find another: NEVER SO MAD A LADIE!

While Dame Eleanor was thus dissuaded from wordplay, the seventeenth century was a great time to be deft with the lexicon. Louis XIII was offering £1,200 a year for the post of Royal Anagrammatist. Too much? By the modern era, it was all a bit much for some. The satirist Jonathan Swift included a credulous approach to the supra-meaning of anagrams among the many targets of *Gulliver's Travels*, deriding those in the kingdom of Tribnia (itself an anagram) for seeking to find evidence of plots in 'the anagrammatic method', giving as an example a letter which reads 'our brother Tom has just got the piles', but can be seen as conveying the seditious message 'Resist, a plot is brought home – the tour'.

When fun is poked at you, the best strategy for survival is often to become fun yourself. So it was with the anagram: by Victorian times, it was a mere diversion. Lewis Carroll, whose predilection for playful wordplay

makes him a kind of ur-setter or constructor *manqué* [SEE
1 DOWN], used to lie awake composing amusing anagrams
of the names of notable people. Like anagrammatists
before him, he was looking for the apposite and revealing,
but his intent was humorous rather than divine: William
Ewart Gladstone can be manipulated into I, WISE MR G,
WANT TO LEAD ALL, 'which is well answered', added
Carroll, by the anagram of Disraeli: 'I LEAD, SIR!'

## THE PALINDROME

The clue might read 'Either way it is unacceptable (3, 2)',
for the answer NOT ON. Or 'Gold medal placing either way
(3, 4)', for TOP SPOT. If a word or phrase reads the same
backwards as forwards (or down as up), you can be sure
that a crossword setter will notice and use it in the clue.

And before there were setters, there were other
palindromists. The art of the palindrome is trickier still
than that of the anagram – so tricky that it helped to be
Lord of Evil Arts to manage it. Here's one of Satan's, cited
by Étienne Tabourot in 1585:

> *Signa, te Signa; temere me tangis et angis;*
> *Roma tibi subito motibus ibit amor.*

This complaint was addressed to St Martin, who had
ordered the devil to change into a donkey and carry him to
Rome. It translates as 'Cross, cross thyself; thou plaguest
and vexest me without necessity; for, owing to my exertions,
thou wilt soon reach Rome, the object of thy wishes.'

Terrifying. However, when they're not being hurled at you by the Prince of Darkness, multi-word palindromes like the above can be giddyingly captivating.

And that urge to travel simultaneously in two directions predates St Martin. Indeed, the **ROMA ... AMOR** palindrome had previously been attributed to the ancient Greek poet Sotades. Sotades, by all accounts, could have made a decent living as a crossword setter. Inventive with language? Check. An unfailing ear for *double entendres*? Oh yes: witness his lines about Ptolemy Philadelphus prodding an unholy hole, an allusion to the king having married his own sister. Among Sotades' innovations was a repeated use of palindromes. So adroit was he that the form has been known as the 'sotadic'. Sadly, he used palindromes for obscenity so frequently that 'sotadic' also, the *Oxford English Dictionary* tells us, means 'characterized by a coarseness or scurrility'. So, tantalizingly, Sotades' satirical ways led to Ptolemy Philadelphus having him thrown into the sea, and little now remains of the poet's work.

Riches were not offered to Sotades, or to others who were able to construct these tricky sentences. Since there are far fewer palindromes than there are anagrams, there was no equivalent post of 'Royal Palindromist', and palindromes were, until the seventeenth century, largely the work of poets working in Greek and Latin. In 1614 John Taylor offered 'five shillings apiece' to anyone who could match his line 'which is the same backward, as it is forward': 'Lewd did I live & evil I did dwel.'

Rowman Taylor, who ferried theatregoers across the Thames to visit the Globe, cheats twice here: the

ampersand represents the non-palindromic word 'and',
and 'dwell' had been spelled with two Ls for a long time
before this. However, as author and wordplay fan Dmitri
Borgmann points out, it can be rescued with a bit of
rejigging to 'Evil I did dwell; lewd did I live.'

And it has to be said that the palindrome is more
rarified and constrained than the anagram: good
specimens are rare, within and without crosswords. The
very best do more than play in both directions; they have a
first and second half that seem destined to fit together,
like the one written by recreational mathematician Leigh
Mercer, 'A man, a plan, a canal: Panama'.

There are longer palindromic phrases, to be sure, but it
takes a mathematician, a crossword setter or a Satan to
devise one with a plausible surface reading.

The Panama palindrome is the one to which most refer
when citing those which are pretty much deified – to the
extent of being parodied. The *New Yorker*'s Roger Angell
was a reviver of its spirit and raises a smile with his own
rotator, something of a gag: 'A dog, a plan, a canal:
pagoda'. You might respond to that with a 'mm', or a 'hah',
depending on your taste.

And computer programmer, Dan Hoey, with a little
help from the Unix spelling dictionary, discovered the
543-word variant:

A man, a plan, a caret, a ban, a myriad, a sum, a lac, a liar, a
hoop, a pint, a catalpa, a gas, an oil, a bird, a yell, a vat,
a caw, a pax, a wag, a tax, a nay, a ram, a cap, a yam, a gay, a
tsar, a wall, a car, a luger, a ward, a bin, a woman, a vassal,

a wolf, a tuna, a nit, a pall, a fret, a watt, a bay, a daub, a
tan, a cab, a datum, a gall, a hat, a fag, a zap, a say, a jaw,
a lay, a wet, a gallop, a tug, a trot, a trap, a tram, a torr, a
caper, a top, a tonk, a toll, a ball, a fair, a sax, a minim,
a tenor, a bass, a passer, a capital, a rut, an amen, a ted, a
cabal, a tang, a sun, an ass, a maw, a sag, a jam, a dam, a
sub, a salt, an axon, a sail, an ad, a wadi, a radian, a room,
a rood, a rip, a tad, a pariah, a revel, a reel, a reed, a pool, a
plug, a pin, a peek, a parabola, a dog, a pat, a cud, a nu,
a fan, a pal, a rum, a nod, an eta, a lag, an eel, a batik, a
mug, a mot, a nap, a maxim, a mood, a leek, a grub, a gob,
a gel, a drab, a citadel, a total, a cedar, a tap, a gag, a rat, a
manor, a bar, a gal, a cola, a pap, a yaw, a tab, a raj, a gab,
a nag, a pagan, a bag, a jar, a bat, a way, a papa, a local, a
gar, a baron, a mat, a rag, a gap, a tar, a decal, a tot, a led,
a tic, a bard, a leg, a bog, a burg, a keel, a doom, a mix, a
map, an atom, a gum, a kit, a baleen, a gala, a ten, a don,
a mural, a pan, a faun, a ducat, a pagoda, a lob, a rap, a
keep, a nip, a gulp, a loop, a deer, a leer, a lever, a hair,
a pad, a tapir, a door, a moor, an aid, a raid, a wad, an alias,
an ox, an atlas, a bus, a madam, a jag, a saw, a mass, an
anus, a gnat, a lab, a cadet, an em, a natural, a tip, a caress,
a pass, a baronet, a minimax, a sari, a fall, a ballot, a knot, a
pot, a rep, a carrot, a mart, a part, a tort, a gut, a poll,
a gateway, a law, a jay, a sap, a zag, a fat, a hall, a gamut, a
dab, a can, a tabu, a day, a batt, a waterfall, a patina, a nut,
a flow, a lass, a van, a mow, a nib, a draw, a regular, a call, a
war, a stay, a gam, a yap, a cam, a ray, an ax, a tag, a wax,
a paw, a cat, a valley, a drib, a lion, a saga, a plat,

a catnip, a pooh, a rail, a calamus, a dairyman, a bater,
a canal: Panama.

    This is only half the length of the monster created by
Georges Perec which begins '*Trace l'inégal palindrome.
Neige. Bagatelle, dira Hercule …*', ends '*… Haridelle, ta
gabegie ne mord ni la plage ni l'écart*' and gets close to the
terrifying-sounding 'fifty tomes of Logogriphs, or curious
Palindromes' envisioned by Ben Jonson in his attack on
novelty verse, *An Execration of Vulcan.*

## THE WORD SQUARE

That same **ROMA … AMOR** palindrome had its most
beautiful physical manifestation in Pompeii. There, those
two words formed part of a design that is the link between
the palindrome and the crossword: the word square.
Carved into the wall of the Domus Poppaeorum was:

R O M A
O L I M
M I L O
A M O R

What does it mean? Nobody knows. Perhaps the 'Milo'
lines are a tribute to the sixth century BC athlete Milo
of Croton, who could carry an adult ox on his shoulders.
That's a guess. Whatever the significance of each compo-
nent, there's no argument about the grace with which they
fit together. Even more impressive is:

```
S A T O R
A R E P O
T E N E T
O P E R A
R O T A S
```

It's a palindrome all right, and this time it has a plausible
meaning – 'the sower, Arepo, skilfully guides the wheels'
– that lends itself better than Roma, Milo, etc, to
interpretation, particularly if you allow yourself a bit of
wiggle room. If Arepo is God, and the wheels are
metaphorical, too, the square would convey that the big
guy upstairs has his eye on all of creation.

There are a few problems with this. One is that the God
interpretation is wholly metaphorical and so equally valid
would be any paraphrase where Someone skilfully does
Something to Something Else. The second problem is that
the canny Roman who devised the square may have
invented the letter string **AREPO** to make the whole thing
work, a compromise familiar to many setters.

But to quibble is to miss the point. Like the anagram,
the word square persisted as a source of fascination: if
words could be made to fit together so well, the reason
had to be a good one, and probably divine. Sure enough, if
you stare at the Sator word square, truths reveal
themselves: you can anagram the 25 letters into a plausible
prayer, or find two instances of the first two words of the
Lord's prayer, **PATER NOSTER**, crossing on the 'N.'

Again like the anagram, the supposed otherworldly qualities contained in the word square are replaced as the word square's raison d'être by the challenge of the construction of the square itself. By the nineteenth and early twentieth century, various minds applied themselves to devising plausible squares of greater size. The larger the square, of course, the fewer your options. You might, like Chicagoan puzzler Wayne M. Goodwin, manage a rare nine-by-nine edifice. But use ten letters and you're likely to have to fall back on abstruse or tenuous words.

Smaller word squares were more feasible and could be found in Victorian newspapers and magazines. Sometimes the letters were removed and readers provided with, effectively, a blank grid and clues for the words which ought to fill it. The word diamond was a popular variant, and it's not hard to see the tiny evolutionary leap from that type of puzzle to the first crossword, Arthur Wynne's 'word-cross' [SEE 3 DOWN].

## THE ACROSTIC

The first acrostics to bear the name were the prophecies of the Erythraean Sibyl, a prophetess who wrote verses on leaves, which could be rearranged such that the initial letters conveyed some important message. They were, however, sometimes a little obscure. Acrostics create readability obstacles sometimes: troubles in comprehensibility.

The habit of leaving hidden messages in the first letters of verses can also be found in the Hebrew version of the Old Testament, Latin poems and the runes of the Anglo-Saxon poet Cynewulf. Here again, it's the same story: early acrostics generally revealed the unknowable, the ineffable or the divine; by Victorian times, they were for sport.

Queen Victoria herself was believed to have adored acrostics and was consequently a reason for their widespread appeal. She apparently created the 'double acrostic' below 'for the royal children', whose job as solvers was to answer each clue such that the first, read top to bottom, spelled out a town, and the last letters, bottom to top, what that town was famous for:

|  | The answers are: |
|---|---|
| A city in Italy | NapleS |
| A river in Germany | ElbE |
| A town in the United States | WashingtoN |
| A town in North America | CincinnatI |
| A town in Holland | AmsterdaM |
| The Turkish name of Constantinople | StambouL |
| A town in Bothnia | TorneA |
| A city in Greece | LepantO |
| A circle on the globe | EcliptiC |

It wasn't long before this enthusiasm found itself expressed in the pages of Victorian magazines. The first double acrostic in print was the following, from the *Illustrated London News* of 30 August 1856:

*A mighty centre of woe and wealth;*
*A world in little, a kingdom small.*
*A tainted scenter, and foe to health;*
*A quiet way for a wooden wall.*
*Find out these words as soon as you can, sir,*
*And then you'll have found this Acrostic's answer.*

**The Letters**

*Untax'd I brighten the poor man's home –*
*My wings wave over the beauty's brow –*
*I steal by St Petersburgh's gilded dome –*
*While Bomba's subjects before me bow.*
*A Cook had reason to dread my name,*
*Though I carry the tidings of pride and shame.*

This puzzle was set by the clergyman and humorist Cuthbert Bede. To the twenty-first-century puzzle solver, it's not immediately apparent where to begin. It would help, for a start, if you had the general knowledge expected of an *Illustrated London News* reader of the 1850s – which is when the window tax was abolished, as referenced in the first line of **THE LETTERS**, and when King Ferdinand II was, due to his fondness for bombing his opponents, known as Il Re Bomba, as he appears in line four. It would help even more if the puzzle had letter counts or a grid.

As in the **NEWCASTLE/COALMINES** example, each line of 'THE LETTERS' is a clue to a single word. The first and last letters of these six words, both reading downwards this time, give the solver two new words, which are described in the verse 'THE WORDS' and which are also given in the notes for this chapter.

Like each of the types of wordplay we've been looking at, reproduction in a magazine caused the popularity of the device to accelerate. Double acrostics became a craze that is perhaps hard to credit today. Marion Spielmann's 1895 history of *Punch* tells how Bede received letters about his puzzles from all over the world, 'forwarded to him in packets by rail'.

It was into this passion for puzzles that the crossword stepped, eventually superseding the double acrostic. The latter is something of a relic, chiefly because the surface readings of most clues are impenetrable nowadays, but it's easy to see the appeal of the form. From the verses spring words, and staring at those words in a different way produces two more words, ever present but only revealing themselves through the steady application of the solver.

Finding hidden messages, then, does not have to reveal the divine to be of value. Stripped of their metaphysics and rendered through Victorian mechanical reproduction, these devices still offer up that moment of revelation – but purely for fun. A little bit of magic, literally boxed up for daily consumption in the quotidian wrapping of newspaper.

# The twisting course of the Neva

**'– GET ENUF' (3LW SONG)**

*New York Sun*, 30 May 2008, set by Brendan Emmett Quigley

3LW was a middling R&B trio modelled after Destiny's Child. In 2002 they released a single called 'Neva Get Enuf', which, nowadays, you can safely go a long time without expecting to hear. It's fair to say that the wilfully misspelled title had more appeal to crossword setters than to music fans: two of its three words have letters in unusual places, a quality much admired in crossword circles.

Take the four-letter string **NEVA**. Sometimes the setter needs a word with a V as the third letter, or an A as the fourth, or both – and there just aren't that many words that end -**VA**, hence the frequent appearance in puzzles of the **DIVA**, a level of superstardom that eluded 3LW.

Before 3LW, there was the river Neva, which flows through Russia from Lake Ladoga to the Baltic Sea. That **NEVA** has appeared in many, many crosswords over the past century. In the *New York Times*, it has been clued straightforwardly as 'Gulf of Finland feeder' and, more cryptically, as 'It has banks in St Petersburg'. Russian setters, too, have found a place for its original name, the    .

*cont'd*

**NEVA** has a special place in crossword history: In Arthur Wynne's 1913 'word-cross', [SEE 3 DOWN] one of the down clues reads: '23-30. A river in Russia'.

Crossing nicely with the entries **LION, EVENING, EVADE** and **ARE** is the **NEVA**. Little was Wynne to know that three years later the Neva would achieve greater fame as the body of water in which, according to his legend, the faith healer Grigori Rasputin drowned, having been thrown in by a group of nobles, who also shot and stabbed him, just to be sure.

Even so, Arthur Wynne was not the first to exploit the potential of **NEVA**. Fifty-seven years before, the first published version of the double acrostic needed a word which began with the third letter of **LONDON** and ended with the third of **THAMES** – and, again, there just aren't many words that fit that criterion. For a century and a half, **NEVA** has been a source of comfort to the constructors of word puzzles. Viva the Neva!

# 7

# Best

*The most audacious feat of multimedia crosswording*

The best single puzzle from the first century of the crossword was published in the Sunday edition of *The New York Times* on 16 November 2008. It has a more than passing connection with the episode of *The Simpsons* that was broadcast that night – 'Homer and Lisa Exchange Cross Words' – and the story starts the previous spring.

One of the writer-producers from the *Simpsons* team attended a talk at University College Los Angeles in May 2007. The speaker was Will Shortz, the NYT's crossword editor. Shortz gives a lot of talks about puzzles and is a one-man American institution.

He holds the world's only degree in enigmatology, having had the good fortune to attend Indiana University, which allows students to 'create a multidisciplinary major that addresses issues and explores topics of your own choosing'. He became NYT puzzle editor in 1993 and encouraged more informality and playfulness than his fogeyish predecessor Eugene T. Maleska, doing away with the bulk of arcane references that had become the norm and practically reinventing the American puzzle in the process.

Wordplay in America is concentrated in fewer locations than it is in UK cryptics, so the US has fewer big-name crossword creators, with Shortz unarguably at the top of the pyramid, and not merely because of his custodianship of the much-loved NYT puzzle. Shortz is known to many through his weekend brain-teasers on National Public Radio and his appearances on programmes such as *The Daily Show*. If you're the kind of American who reads the foreign-news section of the paper, or who supports taxation, you probably know the name Will Shortz – and even if you're, say, Frank Sinatra [SEE 8 ACROSS] or a regular joe who prefers a cup of regular joe to a skinny latte, you might well have become hooked into a dysfunctional relationship with this eminent enigmatologist.

Shortz's UCLA talk came in the wake of *Wordplay*, a 2006 documentary about the culture around the NYT puzzle. In the movie, we meet Shortz fans, including satirist Jon Stewart, documentary-maker Ken Burns and alt-feminist band the Indigo Girls; we learn that Bill Clinton had set a special music-themed puzzle; and we get a glimpse of the intense world of crossword

tournaments [SEE 5 DOWN]. *Simpsons* supremo James L.
Brooks was inspired by these scenes and decided to afflict
Lisa with a love of wordplay and send her to a 'Citywide
Crossword Tournament' – hence the meeting that
followed the UCLA talk, at which it was agreed that
Shortz would help out with the story of Lisa's new hobby
and make a cameo appearance. That was nowhere close to
the ambition realized in the broadcast episode but, for the
time being, it was an excellent fit.

In the story, an
irrepressible Lisa becomes
a crossword convert. Her
school superintendent
finds her making crossing
words out of the
playground's hopscotch
squares – a compulsion to
see puzzles where none
exist that is familiar to
solvers old and young –
and he inspires her to
enter a puzzle
tournament. Naturally, she reaches the final. Homer,
gambling in a nearby bar, bets against her and when Lisa
discovers his treachery, we witness some heartbreaking
scenes: Homer is at a loss how to make it up to his
daughter, and a distraught Lisa has given up on solving
altogether. Towards the end of the episode, Marge
suggests that the *New York Times* puzzle might be a
cheering way for Lisa to spend a couple of hours.

Lisa's fire is reignited: 'A couple of hours?! I can do the Sunday puzzle in less than one hour. "Couple of hours"!' – and on completing that day's puzzle in record time, she notices something unusual hidden in the main diagonal: **DUMB DAD SORRY FOR HIS BET.**

Yes, a chastened Homer has persuaded Will Shortz to publish a puzzle with an apology in the form of a secret message. That might seem like a fanciful piece of fiction, but **[SEE 4 DOWN]** advanced-level setters are prone to using the diagonals or perimeters of their puzzles to make political comments, convey birthday greetings or mark the departure of a loved one.

Yet there's another reason why **DUMB DAD SORRY FOR HIS BET** is not unrealistic: it was real. That is, the puzzle that Lisa solves was an actual puzzle, printed in the edition of the real-world *New York Times* that was published on the day of the episode's first broadcast.

This is where Will Shortz went one better than the *Simpsons* team's ambitions. He had commissioned Merl Reagle, one of the NYT's most playful and imaginative setters, to construct the grid. Three decades before, Reagle had gone to an alternative weekly called the *LA Reader* and suggested that they publish some puzzles he'd been compiling. As he approached the building, he was hoping to meet the paper's cartoonist, the then little-known Matt Groening, who of course went on to create *The Simpsons*.

> The day I went into their office the first thing I asked was if Matt was there and the secretary said, '[You] just passed him in the hall.' If I had arrived just 15 seconds

sooner I would've had the chance to meet him and tell him how much I liked his comic and I've always imagined that we would've been at least casual friends from that day on. I can't tell you how often I've thought about those 15 seconds.

In 2008 Reagle made up for this missed opportunity in spades, designing all the puzzles featured in 'Homer and Lisa Exchange Cross Words' – including those Lisa makes from the hopscotch squares. Even though none of the grids appears for long, Reagle was insistent that any solvers among the viewers should feel that the show had taken the trouble to get the crosswords right.

This attention to detail is sadly lacking in most television crossword props. Devoted solvers get used to having the illusion of reality punctured by glimpses of asymmetrical grids or implausible clueing devices, even in programmes and films where the attention to detail is otherwise impeccable. Pity the ardent crossworder when he or she beholds in unbelieving horror the thirteen-by-thirteen grids in *Inspector Morse* or the complete absence of 1 acrosses or 1 downs in espionage series *Rubicon*.

If you want to avoid a subset of your audience drifting off, harrumphing 'Since when did a national newspaper allow two-letter entries?', the lesson is a clear one. When you need a fictional crossword, tell your props master or mistress to subcontract the work to a setter. Any constraint the script might put on them is just the kind of challenge they like, and for no other reason than that they can work within it [SEE 22 DOWN]. At one point in 'Homer and Lisa Exchange Cross Words', Lisa's tournament rival announces: 'I think I'll warm up with a bunch of "Q"s', and dots his competition grid with them. It's a gag, but Reagle constructed a workable grid with 'Q's exactly where the animators had arbitrarily thrown them.

As for the final puzzle, everyone involved was aware that the reveal would be incredible for any viewers who had solved that day's *New York Times* puzzle. The original plan was to hide *Simpsons* references in the completed grid – Lisa in **PALISADE**, Moe in **AMOEBA**, and so on – but the masterstroke was to avoid this (too obvious) and to get solvers working on what they believed was a completely normal Sunday puzzle, and then they would see a Simpson working on the same grid that same evening.

Even in the unlikely event that anyone spotted that message in the diagonal, **DUMB DAD SORRY FOR HIS BET**, it could have meant nothing to anyone who hadn't been working on the show. One of the greatest pleasures in themed puzzles is what crossworders call the 'penny-drop moment', but never before or since has the pleasure been as delayed or as gratifying as watching Lisa mutter some clues you'd solved that morning before realizing that the denouement of the episode has been hiding in plain view.

There is a good overlap between those who solve the NYT on Sundays and *Simpsons* viewers, and minds were undoubtedly fried. The *New York Magazine*'s Nitsuh Abebe was solving while he watched, and says, 'There was this slow and uncanny real-time convergence between the two.' He began to wonder if he was 'just imagining arcane connections between television and reality', and the moment of revelation was 'like being Bruce Willis at the end of *The Sixth Sense*'.

And that was not all. The fictional Reagle adds that Homer also asked him to include an implausibly demanding acrostic relating to a subplot in which Lisa decides to change her surname from Simpson to Marge's maiden name, Bouvier. And the first letters of the clues read, in order: DEAR LISA YOU MAKE ME SO HAPPY REALLY REALLY REALLY HAPPY SORRY HE TOLD ME I NEEDED A HUNDRED FORTY FOUR LETTERS WHAT WAS MY POINT AGAIN OH RIGHT BOUVIER OR SIMPSON I CHERISH YOU.

This idea for the acrostic came from the real-world Reagle; while he might have regretted it when the scriptwriters sent back a message that meant so many clues beginning with the letter Y, the worlds of crosswords and television would be so much poorer without this remarkable feat of construction.

# Perfectly cromulent words

*The Simpsons* has added to the English vocabulary – and therefore to the supply of words that might appear as crossword answers, including **CRAPTACULAR**, which means exactly what it seems to, the all-purpose slur against the French, **CHEESE-EATING SURRENDER MONKEYS** and ...

**Doh!** is defined in *Oxford* as an interjection 'expressing frustration at the realization that things have turned out badly or not as planned, or that one has just said or done something foolish'. Dan Castellaneta, who plays Homer, told *Variety*: 'The D'oh! came from character actor James Finlayson's "Do-o-o-o!" in *Laurel & Hardy* pictures. You can tell it was intended as a euphemism for "Damn!" I just speeded it up.'

**¡ay caramba!** may have originally been a nickname for eighteenth-century flamenco artist Maria Antonia Fernandez, but it is Bart who made it a widespread and handy way of expressing surprise.

Collins dictionary defines **meh** as 'an expression of indifference or boredom', or an adjective meaning 'mediocre or boring'. *Collins* head of content Cormac

McKeown says, 'This is a new interjection from the US that seems to have inveigled its way into common speech over here. It was actually spelled out in *The Simpsons* when Homer is trying to prise the kids away from the TV with a suggestion for a day trip. They both just reply "Meh!" and keep watching TV; he asks again and Lisa says, 'We said, "Meh!" M-E-H, meh!'

If the clueless Ralph Wiggum had only uttered, 'Me fail English? That's **unpossible!**' between c. 1400 and 1660, when the word was, *Oxford* tells us, 'very common', there would have been no irony in his remark; earlier still, the line appears in Piers Plowman 'Poul prouiþ it is vnpossible riche men in heuene'.

The show's most profound contribution to language is **cromulent**: one teacher remarks that she had never heard the word **EMBIGGENS** before moving to Springfield, and another replies: 'I don't know why; it's a perfectly cromulent word. The online resource Dictionary.com added **CROMULENT** to its twenty-first-century lexicon, and with reason: English had been lacking a facetious way of insisting that something is legitimate in order to convey that it isn't …

# Ruled

*What are the laws of crossword setting?*

Once upon a time, there were no rules of crosswording to break. Edward Powys Mathers, known to solvers as Torquemada, was the first setter to use only cryptic clues. He originally set only for a circle of friends, but one of them arranged for a puzzle of his to appear in the *Saturday Westminster* magazine, from where his crosswords moved to Fleet Street. He developed his style in *The Observer* from 1926 and throughout the thirties [SEE 17 DOWN], trying out techniques of wordplay and generally just doing whatever he liked.

When Torquemada died in 1939, his successor was Derek Somerset Macnutt, better known as Ximenes. He adored the *Observer*'s puzzles – but he thought that it was time to tidy and tighten things up.

The difference between their approaches is perhaps unsurprising. Torquemada's day jobs included that of poet; Ximenes was a classics master and it was the orderliness of the grammar guide that he wished to introduce to crosswords, collecting his thoughts in the 1966 book *Ximenes on the Art of the Crossword*. For Ximenes, each clue, rather than providing a new and uncertain challenge, must provide two routes to the answer. There should be a definition and some wordplay, and the wordplay should act as a 'grammatically sound' recipe that tells you what the ingredients are and precisely how to combine them. Each clue should be capable of being parsed, like a line of computer code, say – or, indeed, a line of Latin verse.

What does 'grammatically sound' mean in the context of crosswords? Well, a setter might write a clue (with a surface reading evoking a media executive) in which the words 'Head of Radio' are meant as an instruction to take the first letter of 'Radio': R. Fine. But another setter who used the name of the band Radiohead to do the same job would fall foul of Ximenes. 'Radio's head', yes, but since 'Radiohead' is not a grammatical way of describing R, it's not 'grammatically sound' in a cryptic.

This grammatical correctness must stand both in the apparent sense of a clue and when it is read as an instruction. So 'Help – I am in short commercial' is okay as a surface reading, but if it is also intended to convey 'put the letter I in the word AD', the 'am' is ungrammatical. A ximenean would rewrite it as 'I can be seen in short commercial' to cover both readings.

And, to be truly ximenean, every word in a clue should

make up part of the recipe. No 'to's or 'fro's to make the surface reading smoother unless they are part of the definition, part of the wordplay or a clear way of suggesting how the latter leads to the former.

It's all very precise, and seamless, but there are solvers who don't realize that a clue might have been created this meticulously. Newcomers tend to assume that cryptics are made of a kind of gobbledygook that might reveal the answer if they peer at it for long enough.

And the puzzles they solve might reinforce that sense, since many can be found in broadsheets which have been created by setters known as libertarians. For them, anyone is free to stick to grammatical soundness if they wish, but it's certainly not the law. Libertarians would be happy to use, say, 'lineage' as wordplay for **EAGLE**, among other allusive and gnomic routes to an answer.

There's a temptation to presume that ximeneans are fun-averse prigs devoid of creativity and libertarians rowdy, irreverent yahoos, but neither is the case. The ximenean could well argue by analogy that chess would be less fun if the knights were occasionally allowed to move diagonally. Since games are fun, and games are defined by their rules, then, you might say, no rules = no fun.

The libertarians, meanwhile, have as their figurehead Araucaria. Taking his pseudonym from the monkey-puzzle tree, the Reverend John Galbraith Graham MBE hardly sounds like a troublemaker, but his philosophy of setting is subtly revolutionary:

[I]n my view any clue is legitimate which leads, by whatever route, to an answer which, 80 per cent of the time, can be known to be correct as soon as it appears to the mind; and any word can be legitimately used in the grid which can be so reached.

For libertarians a clue stands up if the solver can see how it leads to the answer. Araucaria and his votaries – who can be most readily found in the *Guardian* and the *Independent* and have included the setters Bunthorne, Enigmatist and Paul – have no more wish to bamboozle the solver than do the ximeneans. Knowing it's correct when you see it is a different but not a bogus way of defining fairness. The libertarians are not saying 'We don't want to be fair'; they insist that there is another way of playing the game.

So, given that the papers do not mark puzzles as 'libertarian' or 'ximenean', where is safe harbour for the solver who has decided that grammatical soundness is something he or she likes the sound of? For starters, there are the puzzles set by Don Manley, whose Don- or Donald-derived pseudonyms include Bradman, Duck, Giovanni and Quixote. They can be found across the broadsheets, and Manley expands on Ximenes' thinking in his own book, *The Chambers Crossword Manual*. For a stiffer challenge, there is Azed. Under his real-world name, Jonathan Crowther, he described his puzzle as follows:

My crossword is not for novices. It caters unashamedly for solvers who relish a stiff challenge and makes free use of obscure and obsolete words (recent puzzles have included, for example, such gems as **INTUSSUSCEPT**, **OBTEMPERATE** and **ZIBET**), but its clues aim to be fair, accurate and witty.

Crowther sets in the *Observer*, whose tough puzzle has the unbroken sequence Torquemada – Ximenes – Azed. It's remarkable that a single crossword series has had only three setters (if you exclude the brief period when Ximenes shared his duties with the Wimbledon referee Frank Burrow and the Eton master B. G. Whitfield). Most newspapers' puzzles have had dozens of setters, with differing styles and frequencies of appearance; with the *Observer*, there's an element of custodianship as well as setting, especially as the puzzle goes back to the beginning of British crosswords. From the birth of the cryptic under Torquemada to the copy of the *Observer* you can go and buy next weekend, it's an institution hidden in a newspaper – and one that since 1939 has been avowedly and unimpeachably ximenean.

The clue-writing is, accordingly, impeccable, but just as important is the newsletter. Not a lot of crosswords come with a newsletter, but Azed's does and it is one to treasure.

The practice began with Ximenes, who circulated notes around the five hundred or so people who successfully completed his puzzles and established membership of what was to become a kind of informal society, with a Ximenes tie for the men, a scarf for the women, and a book-plate for crosswording merit.

When he died in 1971, his wish was that the mantle

would pass to Crowther, who has maintained both the

puzzles and the notes. Once a month and at Christmas, a
puzzle appears in which one clue is indicated by a simple
definition and no wordplay; solvers are invited to send
their suggested clues that would yield the same answer.
The entrants include professional setters, but the winner is
as likely to be a solver who has a penchant for witty
clueing without having made it his or her living; many
Azed followers have been writing clues since the
competition started in 1972.

In the newsletter, known as 'the Azed slip', the genial
but exacting Crowther announces the winner and
discusses the entries, chats about the puzzle and words in
general and mediates and meditates on fairness.

By the year of the crossword centenary, however –
nearly seventy-five years since Ximenes took over from
Torquemada – the question of what constitutes a sound
clue remains far from exhausted. As more clues appear,
there are more opportunities to revisit, retest and refine
Ximenes' rules. In the Azed slip for March 2013, for
example, Crowther addresses another ongoing issue:
whether setters should use a noun to indicate that there is
an anagram, as in 'car crash' for ARC (his answer is largely a
no). He goes on:

> Some setters are unconcerned by such fine points of
> grammatical and syntactical precision (presumably on
> the grounds that the language of cryptic clues is not
> bound by the same rules as 'normal' English), but they
> remain very important for me. As I have written

elsewhere, 'when it comes down to it, it's a case, as always, of saying what you mean' and consequently 'I make it a personal rule to avoid noun anagram indicators at all times.'

The Azed slip, like the *Listener* crossword [SEE 10 ACROSS], is an institution and a community. There is a dinner after every 250 puzzles for the devoted, and the competition has had a quiet effect on the wider world of crosswording through Crowther's encouragement of deft clueing and the feedback he gives. Don Manley calls the tradition 'Azed's Clue-writing School' and cites some of the best clues, including:

**Item gran arranged family slides in (5,7)**

**Stiff collaring, that's my trade – shows what can be done by starch (4–8)**

**Bust down reason (9)**

The setters of those clues include the creator of Inspector Morse and the man who lent his name to the detective [SEE 18 DOWN]. Others who have repeatedly received commendations may not be famous outside of crosswords but are no less worthy of celebration for that. Azed's family of solvers and fellow setters is playful, fiercely competitive and at times seems like a kind of guild of British crosswording.

# The idiosyncratic Crosaire

Whatever their disagreements, the ximeneans and the libertarians agree that the definition generally belongs at either the beginning or the end of a clue and that you should always be able to work backwards from an answer and say precisely why an answer is correct. Neither of these criteria seemed overly to bother Crosaire, however, the first – and until his death in 2012 – and only setter for the *Irish Times*, as indicated by these clues, which do for the cryptic what Flann O'Brien did for the newspaper column:

It's quite right all rite (7)

Is the pest female to a certain extent? I'll say she is! (6)

Like public enemies to quite a pronounced extent (9)

Is one's limb-in-law dead, perhaps? (9)

Allow this to be just about always little hair, by the sound of it (7)

Haha! Hurry along with ten more (3)

What's so offensive below at the South? Bad fish, no doubt (6)

T's three-quarters of one foot (3)

In the ship the sweet little thing begins to be no better than she ought to be (6)

What a fat ram! (6)

As always, it is in high Latin (7)

You may get the point of the southern pun, perhaps (5–4)

# Tongue-Tied

*The metaplasmic mangling of the
Reverend Spooner*

In December 2010 *Today* programme presenter James
Naughtie tried to introduce 'Jeremy Hunt, the culture
secretary'. He got halfway through a version of that
phrase, inadvertently swapped the opening letters of the
words 'Hunt' and 'culture' and collapsed into giggles.
Naughtie described the error as a 'verbal tangle courtesy of
Dr Spooner', and Hunt was presently moved to a post as
health secretary, where such a verbal switch would make
no difference.

Naughtie that day joined a line of BBC blunderers
which includes the pioneering continuity announcer
McDonald Hobley, who famously introduced MP Sir

Stafford Cripps as Sir Stifford Crapps – but can we really blame nineteenth-century Oxford don Dr William Archibald Spooner for all this?

The practice of taking two words and swapping the sounds at their beginnings, or the main vowel sound within them, is now named after him – but mankind started doing this sort of thing long before Spooner was around. In his 1865 dictionary of slang, John Hotten writes about a 'disagreeable nonsense' then in vogue among medical students at London University. The waggish undergraduate habit of referring to a mutton chop as a 'chutton mop' and a pint of stout as a 'stint of pout' was named 'the Gower Street dialect' after the university's location; before this, such mangled phrases were known as 'marrowskies', apparently after a violin-playing Polish count who was two a half feet tall and amused upper-class women with the same kind of wordplay. However, in 1879, as soon as Dr Spooner introduced a hymn as 'Kinkering Kongs their titles take', his fate was sealed. His students began to refer to him as 'the Spoo' and awaited his every gaffe with gusto.

It was a long wait: in fact, Dr Spooner did not perpetrate many eponymous -isms. His biographers and students of language have been unable to verify 'The lord is a shoving leopard', 'Three cheers for the queer old dean', or 'The half-warmed fish in your hearts.' 'You have hissed all my mystery lectures, tasted the whole worm and must leave by the next town drain'? Far, far too good to be true. Even some of the slips of the tongue that are reliably reported have been tidied up for greater effect: his announcement that a bride and groom had been 'loifully jawned in holy matrimony' became in legend the more powerful 'jawfully loined'. The current edition of the *Oxford Dictionary of Quotations* is happy only with the disappointing 'weight of rages'.

So it's tricky not to pity the Spoo. Already an awkward enough fellow that he absent-mindedly poured claret on to a pile of spilled salt (that one does have a reliable witness), he was unable to deliver a lecture on Tacitus or William of Wykeham without feeling that the undergraduates were hoping he might twist a phrase or two to rude or amusing effect. The rambunctious Maurice Bowra recalled in his memoirs:

> Once after a bump-supper we serenaded him and stood outside his window calling for a speech. He put his head out and said, 'You don't want a speech. You only want me to say one of those things,' and immediately withdrew.

In 1912 Spooner visited South Africa and wrote home to his wife: 'the Johannesburg paper had an article on my visit to Johannesburg, but of course they thought me most famous for my Spoonerisms, so I was not greatly puffed up.'

So why was it Spooner who got the blame from Naughtie, rather than Marrowsky or the 'Gower Street dialect'? One difference is that the count and the medical students were deliberately playing games with language, while Spooner's -isms were, in myth and in reality, accidental. Unintended slips of the tongue are funny in a different way, suggesting a cheering, if fanciful way of looking at the man. If Dr Spooner is not to be remembered for his scholarship or his guardianship of New College, then, rather than as an embarrassment, we should think of him as the embodiment of the subconscious bleeding out into the social – a subversive figure who reveals what can happen when language breaks down.

That's how spoonerisms were seen by the early French surrealists, who deliberately switched syllables in their prose to attack the idea that words and sentences have fixed meanings. Marcel Duchamp's *'Esquivons les ecchymoses des Esquimaux aux mots exquis'* has a surface meaning of sorts ('Let's dodge the bruising of Eskimos with exquisite words'), but its real intent is to force the reader to make fleeting connections that would otherwise seem irrational between eskimos and language, language and the body, the body and eskimos ... and so on. Once you unshackle sounds from their apparent meaning, your mind is better able to question the so-called order of the world around you, which, in the experience of the surrealists, had just proved its own nonsensicality in four years of world war. Being French, they also found wordplay *très amusant*.

The descendants of the surrealists, the experimental writers of Oulipo (the *Ouvroir de Littérature Potentielle*, or Workshop of Potential Literature), were equally fond of the device known in French as the *'contrepet'*. Luc

Étienne's *The Art of the Spoonerism* recalled that, during the Occupation, Parisians 'took a special pleasure in seeing under "*Métropolitain*" in their sad underground stations the sacrilegious inscription "*Pétain mollit trop*"'– Pétain is getting too soft. For Étienne, this is as good an example as any of the subversive potential of the spoonerism: 'a weapon of freedom'.

The memoirs of Resistance secret agent Colonel Rémy take a similar joy in recalling how he arranged for the 'prudish' BBC to broadcast French-language radio messages across the Channel, unaware that they contained scurrilous spoonerisms to cheer up the occupied, such as '*Duce, tes gladiateurs circulent dans le sang!*' The Beeb 'would have shuddered at the mere thought of its airwaves being used to disseminate such imagery'. It's safe to say that, in the forties, the BBC had never broadcast anything quite as rude. I would advise the sensitive reader to read on; the rest of you should turn to the Notes for a translation.

In linguistics, too, the spoonerism is more than a passing slip of the tongue. Even though they're emitted in error, reported spoonerisms share many characteristics; they even seem to have a structure. The affected words are always close together and one of the affected syllables is the one which would be stressed in the correct version of the utterance. More often than not, the swap involves an adjective and a noun; more often than by chance, the spoonerized phrase consists of two real words, however nonsensical they are in context. And when the spoonerized words are not real words, they usually sound as if they could be.

Crossword fans are used to the experience of being
baffled by a clue but knowing some of the letters in an
answer thanks to those that cross with it. If you think
that the answer is a word you haven't heard before, it's
a question of making up words in your head that fit.
You concoct something plausibly pronounceable, which
sounds like other words – which seems to be the kind of
thing that's taking place at great speed in spoonerisms.
A spoonerized phrase might lack literal meaning, but it's
never rhythmically clumsy: there's poetry in the poppycock.
You might find that you've said the phrase 'a picky truzzle'
but not 'a wosscrurd': even your errors are made up of
words that are real, or could be in your language.

That's why the best-loved spoonerisms are those which
work just as well as the intended phrase: the writers for
*The Two Ronnies* enjoyed contriving imagery such as
'Would you mind Mia Farrow?', 'The rutting season for
tea-cosies' and 'You're much too titty to be a preacher,'
just as Dr Spooner's students did two generations earlier.
In the crossword century, setters were not slow to pick up
on the potential for puzzles in spoonerisms, and solvers
are nowadays asked to come up with spoonerized phrases
and reverse-engineer the answer. One of the creators of
the cryptic crossword [SEE 17 DOWN], the poet and
translator Edward Powys Mathers, gave a section in his
1934 collection *Torquemada Puzzle Book* to challenges of
the type:

> *When spoonerized:*
> What aid to illumination suggests a slim sorceress?

What famous public house suggests an unkind puppy?
What light opera suggests the Flying Squad?

Answers in the Notes. The puzzle magazine *The Enigma* used to run a form of puzzle which it called a spoonergram, where you replace the capitalized words in a piece of (slightly dodgy) verse with two phrases, one of which is a spoonerism of the other:

(4 5; 4 5)
His pretty love was young, petite.
Her FIRST adorned by silken bow;
They shared Sauternes, their joy complete;
Their kisses had a LAST, you know.

In crossword clues which use spoonerisms, you're typically given two routes to the answer: a definition and a suggestion of a spoonerized version. So *The New York Times* has offered 'Old comic actor's Little Bighorn headline?', 'Controls a prison guard like a pop singer?' and 'Writer-turned-Utah carpenter?', all of them leading to the names of famous people. American spoonerisms are typically playful and pun-like, and played an important part in the humans-versus-machines battle at the 1999 American Crossword Puzzle Tournament. That year, spoonerisms such as 'May I sew you to a sheet' (another one attributed to Dr Spooner) were the reason that a non-human entrant, the computer programme Proverb, slipped down the rankings – spoonerisms made a lot more sense to flesh-and-blood contestants [SEE 20 DOWN].

Azed in the *Observer* has taken the brain-bending

potential of spoonerisms to another level. This barred weekend puzzle (that is to say, no black squares and at the more challenging end of the crossword spectrum) has a recurring strand in which half the clues give a spoonerized version of the definition –

**Tea arranged around noon? Stash cake (4)**

– where 'stash cake' gives ANTE via 'cash stake', and the other half a definition of a spoonerized version of the answer –

**'Stop martyr dead!' That's about me turning saint (8)**

– where 'stop martyr' gives GEMSTONE via 'stem Joan'. Not knowing which is which forces the brain into endless attempts at spoonerisms, a habit which can be hard to shake even once the grid is filled. Your mind keeps on switching the sounds at the beginnings of words, seeking to find one even more pleasing than the mass of spoonerisms in your head: try as you will to escape, you're embroiled in a battle to outdo yourself. It's stuff to top.

# The easiest cryptic device to spot ...

... is the spoonerism. It's one of the least common of the standard types of cryptic clue, partly because it needs flagging. In the Azed clues above, this happens in the preamble that explains the theme; in weekday puzzles, it's done by the presence in a clue of the word 'Spooner'. It's never too tricky then to isolate the definition, leaving you just the enjoyable activity of word-botching. Here are ten of the best:

As Spooner would say, flimsy weapon for urban activities? (9)

So long to Spooner's dog-end? (6–3)

Provisions for picnic? Spooner's didn't include spicy drink (6,5)

Spooner's pet's entry to working-class symbol (4,3)

Spooner's eager budgie, say, gets food (4, 4)

Wind caused by Spooner's French cheese grab (3,6)

Spooner's friend to welcome pages of abuse! (4, 4)

An insect to flit past, according to Spooner (9)

Spooner's 'you're such a gorgeous pipistrelle' – no charge? (4,7)

Xmas stationery split twice for Spooner (4–4)

# Settlers

*The pioneers who anglicized the American crossword*

It is Britain that is most strongly associated with the form of crossword known as the cryptic. It does appear outside the UK, but its other homes – Australia, say, and Canada, Ireland and South Africa – are largely places which have once seen a Union Flag fluttering at some point in their histories.

When it arrived in Britain from America, the crossword was a puzzle in which each clue was a definition of the answer. Serious newspapers and magazines were reluctant to carry something regarded as a trivial and silly pastime, although their immense popularity gave crosswords a certain fiscal appeal. The *Sunday Express* began experimenting with crosswords in 1924, with the *Telegraph* and the *Guardian* following later in the decade.

Happily, others – free-thinking gentlemen with a certain social standing – were looking at these new grids and wondering whether they could be used for more cerebral fun than finding paraphrases. It's not hard to imagine a poet, an author or a teacher seeing the potential in slotting words together; so it was that a few such Britons invented a new kind of crossword – something to which the *Times* and the *Observer*, the *Listener* and the *Spectator* could put their names without shame. The development was messy and piecemeal at the time but, in retrospect, their combined efforts were an act of complete reinvention.

It was a woman, Margaret Farrar, who firmed up the form of the crossword [SEE 3 DOWN] and female editors (especially at the *Telegraph*) and setters would further refine cryptic clueing, but it was men who first settled in Crosswordland and, bringing it all back home, made it a British tradition that seemed to flow seamlessly from a culture of nonsense verse, Latin grammars and Carrollian wordplay.

The first setter to abandon definitional clues containing only a synonym of the answer and set wholly cryptic puzzles was Edward Powys Mathers (1892–1939), who set as Torquemada. Outside the world of puzzling, Mathers was a literary critic and a translator of *The Thousand and One Nights*. He wrote the plays *Love Night* and *Cold Blood* and the titles of his poetry collections, such as *Sung to Shahryar* and *The Smell of Lebanon*, give a sense of his broad, cross-cultural interests.

Understandably, synonyms were, for Torquemada, not nearly stimulating enough: 'too easy to hold for long the attention of anyone concerned with and interested in words'. Between 1926 and his untimely death in 1939 he composed 670 crosswords for the *Observer* in which he reinvented what a puzzle could do.

He popularized puzzles which had a theme uniting many of the entries and used gimmicks, including clues presented as rhyming couplets and knock-knock jokes, for instance, 'Blank who? Blank'd love to (7)'. Most of all, he initiated the practice in crosswords of eliciting an answer by means of the letters the clue contains as well as its literal meaning.

Mathers set under a pseudonym, a practice since followed by most British setters since, with the exception of the *Sunday Times* (real names) and the *Times* and *Telegraph* (anonymous). Some thought he did so to protect his literary reputation; others took it as a sign of his playfulness. Mathers took his *nom de guerre* from a vicious Grand Inquisitor of the Spanish Inquisition. That would nowadays be termed 'inappropriate judgement', but it seemed appropriate to his followers, who had to become used to an intensely idiosyncratic style in which you never knew what you were going to get. For example, in 'Creeper formed of Edmund and his son Charles (5)', you have to guess that you are being asked to take the surname of the actors Edmund and Charles Kean, then pluralize and anagrammatize it for SNAKE, defined as 'creeper'. Cryptic clues would become less wayward, but this was an audacious and irresistible start.

Mathers' widow remembered him thus: 'I see him sitting cross-legged in bed, with a puzzle in front of him, looking very like a somewhat relaxed Buddha, a cigarette between his fingers and eyes fixed in the distance – until something clicks and, with a contented smile or discontented shrug, he writes on the list in front of him, and ticks off the word in gaily coloured chalk.'

Another pioneer preferred the great outdoors when composing clues. Adrian Bell (1901–80) was the son of Robert Bell, the news editor of the *Observer*. Bell Junior did a short stint at that paper before a recurrent migraine persuaded him to take up a position as a farm apprentice in Suffolk. He then bought his own farm and while tending it wrote about rural life and celebrated pre-mechanical agriculture, starting with the trilogy *Corduroy*, *Silver Ley* and *The Cherry Tree*.

Bell said of his own writing that he wanted 'to put into words the way unrelated things came together and formed a relation', which was just as well, when the job of crossword setting was imposed on him in 1930.

In December 1929, *Times* editor Robert Barrington-Ward had been jealously eyeing the popularity of the *Telegraph*'s crossword. He was friends with Bell Senior, whose paper had been publishing Torquemada's intelligent puzzles for four years and asked for a suggestion as to who could provide something for the *Times*:

> So then my father came to me. We were sitting in the country, trying to farm with a pair of horses, and he said, 'Look, my boy, you're going to make up crossword puzzles for the *Times*.'

'But Father,' I said, 'I haven't even solved a crossword puzzle.'

'Well', he said, 'you've got just ten days to learn!'

Adrian Bell, talking to the BBC

Paid three guineas per puzzle, Bell learned fast, and many of the all-time most-loved clues have been attributed to him, including 'This cylinder is jammed (5, 4)'; 'Die of cold (3, 4)'; and 'Spoils of War (4)'. Essentially, his task was to provide challenges which would not 'affront the dignity' of upper-crust *Times* readers, and the crosswords were originally printed only in the weekly, non-UK edition of the paper, to diminish the shock of the inclusion of puzzles in the national journal of record.

The typical *Times* solver was assumed, in the words of the paper's current crossword editor, Richard Browne, to have 'graduated from governess to public school to Oxford and Cambridge'. That was not the case for Bell himself. His son, the journalist and former MP Martin Bell, thinks that not having been to a university made him a better setter: 'He had a totally free, unchannelled mind with a lot of stuff in it, and a lot of stuff is what he put in his puzzles.'

For Bell himself, it became 'the ideal job for a chap with a vacant mind sitting on a tractor harrowing clods or bicycling', and he created something like three thousand puzzles, his last being the *Times*' ten-thousandth, printed shortly before his death in 1980.

The argument that a classical education is, in fact, no impediment to the setter is made by the career of Derrick

Somerset Macnutt (1902–71), who had gained a
scholarship to Marlborough College and another to Jesus
College, Cambridge, where he won three prizes and left
with a double first. In the world of classics, Macnutt is
well remembered for the 1939 Latin course and grammar
he co-wrote with H. L. O. Flecker. In the world of
crosswords, he was Ximenes.

Macnutt was a devotee of Torquemada's puzzles and,
when Mathers died, he sent the *Observer* a tribute puzzle.
This was well received; Macnutt was asked to take over
Mathers' duties, and chose the name of the real-world
Torquemada's successor: Francisco Jiménez de Cisneros,
or Ximenes.

Again, the sadistic moniker was apt, though for
different reasons: Macnutt's day job was senior classics
master at Christ's Hospital, where he was known for his
keenness for corporal chastisement, as well as for wearing
pebble glasses and plus fours and for smoking five ounces
a week of flake-tobacco.

Macnutt maintained the *Observer*'s puzzle for over
three decades, and set 1,200 crosswords as Ximenes, as
well as some of the *Observer*'s less demanding Everyman
and some of the more exacting challenges in the *Listener*,
as Tesremos (his middle name in reverse). As Ximenes, he
was innovative and collaborative. The innovations included
'misprint' clues in which the solver assumes there is a
single-letter mistake; and the collaboration took the form
of readers' clue-setting competitions.

Most important was his refinement of Torquemada's
erratic approach. While he said of setting that 'you have to

be a lunatic with a distorted mind to do it,' he was
insistent that that distortion be governed by rules of
grammar and parsimony [SEE 13 DOWN], which he
elaborated at length in his 1966 book *Ximenes on the Art of
the Crossword*.

In Ximenes clues such as 'Tay sure may be seen to
emerge in one (7)' and 'An important city in
Czechoslovakia (4)', you can be sure that there is not a
single extraneous word and, while many subsequent setters
have chosen not to follow all of his edicts, his emphasis on
fairness is shared by all and was to crosswording's
immense benefit. His final puzzle was published
posthumously in 1972.

Two other classics teachers shared Macnutt's passion
for codification. Three chapters of *Ximenes On the Art of
the Crossword* were written not by Ximenes but by the
setter known at the *Guardian* as Custos and in the
*Listener* as Zander: Alec Robins (1917–98). Robins taught
at Chorlton and Stand grammar schools and went on to
write 1975's popular how-to book *Teach Yourself Crosswords*.

The other classicist was Alistair Ferguson Ritchie
(1890–1954), the son of a post-office clerk who went on to
become head boy of his grammar school and took holy
orders after graduating from Queens' College, Cambridge.
He became the headmaster of Wells Cathedral School
and prebendary of the cathedral itself, but took the unholy
name of Afrit for his crosswords. An afrit is a powerful
and cunning Arabic demon which can be found in *The
Thousand and One Nights* and the Koran, as well as in the
name A. F. Ritchie.

Ritchie placed great importance on the school's croquet lawn (where he was usually the victor) and beehives (where he usually got stung). He was also a keen solver: having won the *Observer*'s prize so many times that he became ineligible, he began to enter using the names of his colleagues and, later, the pupils, one of whom remembered being told by Ritchie: 'Congratulations, you won the *Observer* crossword prize last week. Would you be good enough to let me have it some time?'

Like Ximenes, Afrit invented many cryptic devices. He set frequently for the *Listener* between 1932 and 1948, concocting such exoticisms as Printer's Devilry, Playfair and Word Ladder. And, again like Ximenes, the most important part of his legacy is his advice to other setters. A cryptic clue lacking a definition would be near unimaginable now, but Ritchie thought it needed spelling out. 'There must be a clue to the meaning of the whole word,' he insisted. 'If the composer can't sustain his amusing idea without breaking this rule, let him think again and not expect to score so cheaply.'

This, along with other gentle admonitions, is from the introduction to his 1949 collection *Armchair Crosswords*, which also contains the *ne plus ultra* of crosswording counsel: Afrit's Injunction [SEE 1 DOWN].

The actual clues of Afrit puzzles have an unfamiliar look to the modern-day solver, chiefly because of their length. The same goes for our other pioneers, at times more literary, more difficult or more prone to knock-knock puns than contemporary setters. But they are certainly recognizably cryptic and they mark the introduction of a new kind of fun to the puzzle devised in 1913. Steeped in British tradition but unapologetically modern, the cryptic gave fresh life to the acrostics, anagrams and other forms of wordplay [SEE 6 DOWN] that long predated it.

# Gegs?

Often, people say that their favourite – or indeed the best – cryptic clue is this: 'Gegs (9, 4)'.

This is possibly due to an episode of newsroom sitcom *Drop the Dead Donkey*, in which the irascible journalist Henry spends days stuck on the clue, allegedly from the *Sunday Times*. '"Gegs!"' he barks. 'What the hell sort of a clue is that?'

The answer is: not a cryptic one, not really. Cryptics typically offer two routes to the answer; 'Gegs' offers none. The answer given is **SCRAMBLED EGGS**, so if you were being kind, you might say that really the clue should be the answer, and the answer part of the clue – except that most newspapers would consider the answer **GEGS** (a nineteenth-century variant spelling of a word for a member of an Albanian people living mainly in northern Albania, Kosovo and western Macedonia) too obscure.

More importantly, 'Gegs' makes sense only when you know the answer. This makes it a poor ambassador for crosswords, though this kind of backward-working clue was once occasionally seen. In 1963, *Telegraph* setter Douglas St Paul Barnard describes it as the 'Parabolic Clue' and advises sparing use: 'they are rich fare, and like Marmite: "Too much spoils the flavour."'

He does, however, see the Parabolic as a bulwark against 'the impressive strides now being made in the manufacture of electronic computers', challenging anyone who wishes to programme a crossword-solving machine to 'feed into his *machina sapiens* the clue "No adequate description of father's cuemanship (4)"'.

He adds in an antsy footnote: 'I do not give the answer to this clue lest our hypothetical programmer should "build" the solution into his machine. I can only vouch to its being absolutely fair.'

Since Barnard adds that 'should any particularly astute solver think that he has just seen the answer, let me assure him that he is right,' it appears that the clue is supposed to indicate **FAIR**, possibly because father (**FR**) has got a first-class (**A1**) break. Gosh. Too much spoils the flavour indeed.

# Whodunit

*Crosswords and detective fiction*

'It's all clues, isn't it? Crosswords are far more exotic
and exciting than police work. Most murders don't
require solving because they haven't been planned.'

— Chief Inspector Morse, *The Settling of the Son*

The crossword took off at the same time as the whodunit
and the jigsaw. It's tempting to explain the appeal of all
three puzzles by some primeval urge to solve, but that type
of explanation raises more questions than it answers –
which may be the sign of a good puzzle but is also
indicative of a bad piece of analysis. Attributing action to
a 'need' does no more than restate its existence.

Certainly, there's an overlap between these forms
of puzzle. Georges Perec set crosswords for *Le Point*

newspaper and frames his experimental novel *La Vie*
*mode d'emploi* using jigsaws; the pioneering cryptic setter
Torquemada [SEE 17 DOWN] reviewed 1,200 detective novels
over four years; and Edgar Allan Poe, the godfather of the
mystery story, concealed such elaborate messages in his
poetry that some verses were practically double acrostics.

For some commentators, what all these forms of puzzle
have in common is that they are a waste of time. A. J. P.
Taylor finds a little value in detective fiction for providing
'accurate social detail' for the historian of the period, then
dismisses the genre as '[otherwise] without significance:
an intellectual game like the crosswords, which became a
universal feature in the newspapers at this time'. A. N.
Wilson goes further:

> The cryptic crossword and the whodunit mystery story
> were two distinctive products of their time, expressions
> no doubt of the belief that if one could only worry at a
> problem for long enough it would have a single simple
> solution: Keynesian or Marxist economic theory,
> Roman Catholic, communist or fascist doctrine.

The connection sounds neat enough, but it doesn't stand
up. Cryptic crosswords are the very opposite of simplistic:
their whole appeal is based on the ambiguity of language.
Wilson is no solver, though, as evidenced by the inclusion
in his biography of John Betjeman a letter apparently
written by the poet to his mistress. The document was a
hoax, and the first letters of its sentences – 'All day, I've
thought of nothing else. No other love I've had means so
much …' – spelled A. N. WILSON IS A SHIT. The hoaxer's

identity remains unknown; like in a classic mystery story, the plausible suspects are legion.

Even among defenders of the whodunit, there are those who make similar attacks on the crossword. Stung by the idea that their love of genre fiction indicates a feeble mind, these mystery fans grant that yes, there is a subgenre called the howdunit, which is as shallow and abstract as a mere crossword puzzle, but the books *they* read are all about flawed protagonists and social satire and accurate forensics and yada yada yada.

The mistake here is in thinking that there's anything to be gained in distancing yourself from those apparently simpler mystery tales. Moreover, the 'crossword' genre is as diverse as the whodunit: some locked-room mysteries provide fast, single-solution diversion, as do some concise crosswords; some golden-age detective novels abound in red herrings, as do some cryptics; private-eye stories, like American puzzles, might boast an extended range of personalities and cultural detail; historical detectives, like themed cryptics, may exploit the pleasures of arcane specifics ... but perhaps the best analogy is not between a story and a puzzle, but between a story and a clue.

In 1968 Stephen Sondheim wrote a piece for the magazine *New York* which attempted to convince American crossword solvers to try British cryptics. The article's subtitle, 'What's A Four-Letter Word for "East Indian Betel Nut" and Who Cares?', gives a sense of his argument: Sondheim characterizes American puzzles as full of 'bald definitions' and praises the bafflement offered by the surface readings of cryptics.

'A good clue,' Sondheim insisted, 'can give you all the pleasures of being duped that a mystery story can.' Among those pleasures are apparent innocence, surprise and the catharsis of exposing what has really been going on.

The setter as whodunit-writer? There is a certain affinity. Both, if they wish to dodge charges of unfairness, must give all the necessary information such that the 'solution' will make sense in retrospect. Both must avoid making this too obvious, and both are probably more prone to making it too arcane. Novice setters have a tendency to write clues which make perfect sense to themselves but prove impenetrable to solvers. And Agatha Christie seemed to be talking about her own craft in the story *Why Didn't They Ask Evans?* when she had Lady Frances Derwent muse on a clue to a murder given by another character. 'It's like making crossword puzzles,' she remarks. 'You write down a clue and you think it's too idiotically simple and that everyone will guess it straight off, and you're frightfully surprised when they simply can't get it in the least.'

And then there's the solver as sleuth, a correspondence seen in detective fiction from its beginnings to the present day. In Alan Plater's whodunit *Oliver's Travels*, the detective is of the amateur variety: Oliver is a recently fired lecturer in comparative religion who is intrigued by the disappearance of Aristotle, his favourite setter. At the end of a picaresque hunt, Oliver is told that he, like Aristotle, has 'an inventive and lateral mind – no use in a straight line, but brilliant sideways'. In these stories, there is an overlap between understanding clues and understanding the world: both demand of you a scepticism regarding first impressions and invite you creatively to suggest connections that might at first appear to defy common sense.

Oliver's journey from Rhondda to Orkney is punctuated by his daily hunt for a copy of the *Guardian*, and the clues in the paper's crossword inform his quest as he stumbles on to a few murders, some arson and a nasty conspiracy.

Given that Plater wrote the introduction to a collection of puzzles by the real-world *Guardian* setter Araucaria (and once met him in the garden of jazz clarinettist John Dankworth), it's impossible not to read *Oliver's Travels* as a love letter to Araucaria and to cryptic thinking in general.

The Britain through which Oliver travels is a mad world, where mercenary and mercantile disruption masquerade as rational calculation. Rather than subscribe to specious logic, Oliver prefers to hand over his love life and his safety to decisions based on wordplay.

Plater's story is a homage to unorthodox reasoning, playfulness and thinking things through slowly; to those who suspect that crosswords shut out experience and feeling, *Oliver's Travels* insists that solving is just those things.

In the BBC adaptation, Oliver's love interest, WPC Diane Priest (she introduces herself as 'Diane, not Priest' and Oliver believes in **PREDESTINATION**), solves while Oliver drives, entering at 9 across what looks very much like **MORSE**, the detective whose name is even more crosswordy than one derived from an anagram.

In the early 1970s, before they had become an uptight, morose inspector and his looser colleague, Morse and

Lewis were the real-world names of a chairman of Lloyds Bank and a crossword setter. Sir Christopher Jeremy Morse and Mrs B. Lewis were frequent entrants in and winners of the monthly clue-writing competition that accompanies the *Observer*'s august Azed crossword [SEE 13 DOWN]. Mrs B. Lewis wasn't strictly allowed to enter, as she was in reality Dorothy Taylor, who set for the same paper's Everyman puzzle, hence her use of a pseudonym.

These solvers-turned-clue-setters were known to each other through the newsletter in which Azed announces the winners and discusses crosswording in general. In June 1976 he observed that regular entrants might have noticed 'the disappearance from these lists for some time of N. C. (Colin) Dexter, for many years a redoubtable competitor'.

Dexter is redoubtable as crossword evangelist as well as competitor, as seen in his book for solvers, *Cracking Cryptic Crosswords*. He became enamoured of cryptics during the Second World War when he read a clue in the *News Chronicle*: 'Ena cut herself (7)'. It's a poor clue for ENABLED, one which lacks definition, and Dexter himself would go on to write much more pleasing examples, such as '(Biol.) Treat defective end of a tube (10)'.

Azed reassured the reader that Dexter was alive and well but had temporarily foresworn crosswords for 'clues of another kind'. More specifically, he had been writing the first two Inspector Morse novels, *Last Bus to Woodstock* and *Last Seen Wearing*. He has since said that he regarded Morse and Lewis as 'distant heroes' at the time, and that 'it seemed only natural to choose Morse and Lewis, two names that had become such a big presence in my life, as the names for the two key figures.' With the exception of the murderer, every character in *Last Bus to Woodstock* gets his or her name from one of the *Observer*'s setters and solvers.

Crosswords don't just lurk behind the scenes in Morse, of course. The first meeting of the fictional Morse and Lewis takes place over a clue. Lewis, a *Mirror* coffee-time crossword man, is confronted by Morse thrusting a paper at him and instructing him to look at 14 down: 'Take in bachelor? It could do (3)'. He is no less puzzled when Morse explains why the answer is BRA, so when his superior asks 'Do you think I'm wasting your time?' and he answers 'Yes, sir,' it's clear that the partnership is going to work.

Like Oliver, Morse later explains that his way of solving is sideways: 'The trouble with my method, Lewis, is it's inspirational. And as a result, I sometimes – sometimes – get things arse-about-face.' And, like Oliver, he sometimes finds that his moments of inspiration come while solving. This is especially the case when some piece of evidence contains an acrostic or similar, but in *The Silent World of Nicholas Quinn*, it's the tone of a clue that sets him off.

While trying to work out which of the suspects in a murder case might have visited a cinema to see a pornographic film, Morse takes an impressive twelve and a half minutes [SEE 5 DOWN] to solve the *Times*: he would have been within ten minutes but for the clue 'In which are the Islets of Langerhans (8)', for which he has —A—C—E—S.

When the inspector twigs that the setter is trying to

make him conjure up a sea which fits those letters rather than **PANCREAS**, he sees that the suspects had been acting like a crossword setter: trying to make him work out who had been in the cinema, when nobody had been there at all. In the television adaptation of the story, written by keen solver Julian Mitchell, one of the suspects is actually a setter: the fiendish Daedalus, who tells Morse: 'I do try to be just a little bit cleverer than the solver, you see. I always try to make 5 down just a little tricky.'

Daedalus meets an end so grisly that even frustrated solvers who have wished misfortune on real-life Daedaluses would probably consider a bit strong: he is bludgeoned to death. Happily, Morse solves the case, proving that, without his love of crosswords, the sitting rooms and common rooms of Oxford would be littered with even more cadavers.

Morse's tastes tend to the *Times* and the *Listener* [SEE 10 ACROSS], but there's an attraction to picturing him solving the real-world cryptics in the *Oxford Times* that were set by his creator. Dexter's puzzles are elegant packages of wit and wordplay which would have suited the inspector well over a lunchtime pint or three at the Lamb and Flag. He would have been hard-pressed, though, to see the hidden messages in the *Times* puzzle of 18 March 1993. Inspector Morse's world is one where there is surely no *Inspector Morse* on TV, and so the names of the series' composer, lead actor and creator would mean nothing to him.

| D | E | B | A | R | R | I | N | G | | T | O | N | D | O |
|---|---|---|---|---|---|---|---|---|---|---|---|---|---|---|
| I | | U | | E | | D | | I | | O | | I | | R |
| S | T | R | O | P | H | E | | L | O | U | N | G | E | D |
| C | | N | | A | | A | | L | | R | | H | | E |
| R | I | S | E | R | | L | E | I | C | E | S | T | E | R |
| E | | | | T | | I | | E | | R | | G | | |
| D | I | S | P | E | R | S | E | | | | J | O | H | N |
| I | | T | | E | | T | | C | | B | | W | | E |
| T | H | A | W | | | G | O | V | E | R | N | O | R | |
| | G | | B | | A | | V | | R | | | | | V |
| C | I | G | A | R | E | T | T | E | | L | O | D | G | E |
| O | | E | | A | | H | | R | | I | | R | | L |
| M | O | R | O | C | C | O | | L | I | N | E | A | G | E |
| I | | E | | E | | M | | E | | E | | C | | S |
| C | E | D | E | D | | E | X | T | E | R | I | O | R | S |

# Superstates

Sondheim's depiction of American puzzles as merely definitional should not deter British solvers. The cryptic definition [SEE 12 ACROSS] is a type of clue which is found more often in US puzzles than it is in the UK and – whisper it – the Americans are better at it. Here are ten, with British-style letter counts added:

Early summer? (6)

Fits on a hard drive? (4, 4)

Letters from your parents? (3)

Pecking order? (4, 2)

Response to getting a ring? (5)

Public hangings? (3)

Full of life? (8)

Dangers for the over-70 crowd? (5, 5)

Cover of the Bible? (3, 4)

Place that British women can't stand going? (3)

# Enigma

*Can machines do crosswords?*

Solving a cryptic clue makes you feel good. You've been given a sentence with an apparent meaning and you've teased out its hidden message. It feels creative, thoughtful.

Take a clue like 'Tear off, certain to find riches (8)'. The surface reading is of someone dashing away following a tip-off about a pot of gold. But you know better: 'off' looks like a word that indicates an anagram, so we might have an anagram of the word before it ... that would mean the definition comes at the other end of the clue ... yep, 'to find' is probably a linking phrase between the wordplay and the anagram ... aha, so it's an anagram of 'tear' plus a word for 'certain' that makes up a word for 'riches'... **TREA** plus **SURE** equals **TREASURE**. Got it!

It's humbling, then, to look at the following piece of output from a computer programme written in a language called **LACROSS** ('**LA**nguage for **CROSS**-word puzzles') by P. W. Williams and D. Woodhead. So, here's a human typing in a clue for **LACROSS** to solve:

ENTER CLUE
? TEAR OFF, CERTAIN TO FIND RICHES.

**LACROSS** looks at 'off' and identifies it as one of the words that tends to indicate an anagram, so it marks it with an 'A'.

OFF   POSSIBLE COMPONENTS/   OPERATORS – A

**LACROSS** looks at 'find' and identifies it as a word which might connect the wordplay with the definition, and marks it with an '='.

FIND   POSSIBLE COMPONENTS/   OPERATORS – =

**LACROSS** runs through synonyms for 'riches' and words which begin with an anagram of 'True' and chooses **TREASURE**, which fits every part of the clue. It's a fast solve, and it didn't need today's processing power: that clue was solved in 1977.

ANSWER = TREASURE –
   anagram of TEAR + SURE for 'certain'

It was a very promising start for automaton solvers – and they have come on in the three decades since. The most prominent of the current crossword bots is called Dr Fill (a pun on Phil McGraw's psychology TV show *Dr Phil*). Dr Fill was created by former artificial-intelligence researcher Matt Ginsberg, who runs algorithms for the US Air Force when he isn't setting *New York Times* puzzles. For portability, he wanted his machine to be small, so he loaded up a MacBook Pro laptop with the code he'd created. He added pre-existing crossword answers dating back to 1990 and chunks of resources such as Wikipedia and the Internet Movie Database, and took it along to the 2012 American Crossword Puzzle Tournament [SEE 5 DOWN].

Dr Fill was not an official entrant: one of the requirements for entry to the tournament is that you are a person. If a person had performed the same as Dr Fill, he or she would have come 140th – not a bad placing, and one that can only improve as more time and human thought goes into the software.

Ginsberg, though, doesn't think that what Dr Fill does counts as thinking. It is, he says, a serial business of summoning likely answers and seeing whether they fit with each other. 'Thinking' or not, that's a pretty good description of how most humans approach most quick crosswords and of some of the techniques that help finish off a cryptic. There is, though, something missing from Dr Fill's approach, something which should become more apparent as it learns from its mistakes – and that's a discipline it's certainly more serious about than many of its biped rivals.

A hint as to what that missing element might be came when the 2012 Tournament included an unexpected twist in one of the puzzles, whereby some answers had to be entered unconventionally. A human might wonder for a

while what is going on when the answer **MOON MISSIONS**
doesn't seem to fit the squares for 'Apollo 11 and 12 [180
degrees].' But once you twig what '180 degrees' is asking
for and see that **SNOISSIWNOOW** fits with the crossing
answers, you can enter it with the kind of confidence that
a machine isn't going to have unless it's been given a line
of code which explicitly says that 'W's can be exchanged
for 'M's under certain conditions.

And while adding such extra possibilities is not an
insurmountable technical problem, that moment of
realization is where automated solvers begin to part
company with their flesh-and-blood rivals. For Dr Fill, this
would be merely another device in the armoury. For human
solvers, there's something endearingly daft about entering
an answer the wrong way up, the words hanging upside
down like a spaceman on a moon mission. Computers will
make qualitative progress in tone, speed, range, and so on
– but there's something spooky about giving them clues
whose whole purpose is a silliness and humour which they
seem eternally unlikely to be able to enjoy.

Perhaps there's a better job for technology in creating
puzzles rather than solving them. While the range of
available grids was once determined by the lead blocks
from which the squares were printed, that job is now done
by the software used by the setters, editors and printers of
British broadsheet puzzles.

Crossword Compiler is an impressive, versatile
programme that allows setters to save their puzzle in a
form that takes it seamlessly to its spot in the paper, down
to the brackets indicating the length of the answers. Its

creator, Antony Lewis, is a Brighton-based astrophysicist (and, being a caring type, he offers a discount on the licence to any user who promises that they take at most two flights in any twelve-month period).

The first of the many choices it offers the setter is an array of grid types: American or British, barred or blocked, twenty-eight, thirty or thirty-two answers, and so on. It certainly gets you to the fun part more quickly: you can be concocting amusing cryptic definitions in seconds without any time spent peering at graph paper or blocking out a symmetrical arrangement.

Some take comfort in the assumption that this kind of architectural donkey work might be the extent of computers' involvement in setting. In 1984 Tony Augarde wrote in *The Oxford Guide to Word Games* that it seemed unlikely that computers could be programmed to construct clues showing 'ingenuity'; in 2003 former *Sunday Times* crossword editor Barbara Hall told the BBC that she thought a further impediment would be the size of the word bank the machine would require, 'because there are so many different meanings for one word'.

However, in technical terms, there's barely a difference between a 'word bank' of a few thousand words and one of a couple of hundred thousand. And Crossword Compiler doesn't stop at grid construction. If you ask it to, it will fill the grid with words. And, it will examine it and tell you what a certain word is an anagram of, whether you can add a letter to make it an anagram of something else, and so on. As soon as you look at the suggestions, the clueing is halfway done.

And if you want it all the way done, there's another programme. Enigma leads the field in terms of wholly machine-generated clueing. Written by David Hardcastle, for any answer, the software generates a list of 'clue plans': the anagrams, reversals, soundalikes, and so on, that can be combined to clue it.

For each device, it suggests how a certain anagram, reversal or soundalike might be indicated. The number of possibilities for any given answer is enormous. In addition, Hardcastle is keen that the clues generated by Enigma should have 'a valid puzzle reading and a fluent surface reading', citing the criterion of *Observer* setter Azed: it must resemble a plausible piece of English prose. Happily – perhaps – there's a digital approach to this problem.

The British National Corpus is a 100-million-word collection of real-world examples of spoken and written English. It was assembled by three dictionary publishers, two universities and the British Library, and it aims to store English in machine-readable form. Enigma takes the words in a possible clue and uses the BNC to check how often they are frequently found together as a means of assessing the plausibility of the surface reading.

Some of the resulting clues read very well. 'Notice that large noses are runny' is eminently plausible as a piece of English prose, though there are better definitions of LESSON than 'Notice'. But the approach has its drawbacks. Experimenting with the programme, crossword blogger Shuchismita Upadhyay requested suggested clues for VIEWERS. Enigma could see that the word could be indicated as ER inside an anagram of WIVES, and the word it suggested to indicate the anagram was 'battered'. 'Battered wives' might well be a plausible word-pair, but it's not an image that anyone wants to contemplate during a solve.

There is probably no reason for us to expect to see computer-set puzzles in the newspapers any time soon. This is not because of misjudged clues like 'battered wives': it's by no means beyond the capabilities of a programme to allow for tone and offence – Enigma just needs more data.

The real reason is the way a solver typically conceives of the challenge of a given grid and set of clues. It's not an abstract mass-produced means of whiling away some minutes but a contest between two people, the setter and the solver, where the solver knows that the setter has conceived of the grid as a whole, balanced in terms of tone, subject matter, technique and difficulty.

More importantly, the setter's role is, in a phrase much beloved of solvers and setters, to 'lose gracefully': to guess correctly that the solver will, with enough application, find the wherewithal to topple every clue and fill every square. Each setter's idea of what the solver is likely to know differs, based on hunches and experience – and those differences are as good a way as any of defining the varying personalities among setters. It's with setters' personalities that solvers make the relationships that keep them coming back. 'I beat Taupi today' means something qualitatively different to 'I beat *Daily Sketch* Midweek-Bot v2.1'. And, once a solver has found the newspaper that suits them, they've made a relationship with a kind of gang – and a gang of highly characterful and diverse individuals who share an ethos that's different if you're a daredevil *Independent* solver to the one you share if you're a steady, sturdy *Times* devotee.

Setting is regarded by solvers as a kind of authorship, and our relationship with an author is dependent on their being a person too. The editors of the *Daily Telegraph* discovered this in 1998 when they initiated a scheme to automate crossword production. Humans would still be paid to write clues, but at that point they would enter a database from which each day's puzzle could be assembled.

The ostensible reason was to reduce the frequency with which some words appeared as answers, although there was also an undeniable financial incentive. A core of the setters refused to play ball and became known as the '*Telegraph* Six'. Ruth Crisp (Crispa) gave her withering assessment of the wheeze: 'I don't think a crossword done on a computer can possibly compare with one done individually. I have been compiling crosswords for half a century and I think my judgement can be depended on.'

The invisible symmetries of human arrangement could not be replicated by machine, she insisted, and Roger Squires (Rufus) predicted that the tone of the resulting puzzles would be 'like combining the musical styles of Beethoven and Mozart in the same musical movement'. This in a newspaper with anonymous setters.

The paper's deputy editor, Boris Johnson, was forced to agree. 'In spite of the advantages the computer possesses, the machine has been condemned for a fatal lack of soul,' he announced. 'The crossword will remain a duel of wits between the individual composer and the solver.' Squires responded with a single clue – 'Submit to pressure and return to base (9)' – and returned to business.

# Decryptic

As part of the evaluation of his Enigma software, David Hardcastle subjected some of the programme's clues to a Turing test: can a human distinguish the machine-written clues from those composed by flesh-and-blood setters?

He assembled thirty pairs of clues: each pair shared an answer and, in each pair, one was from the *Sun's* cryptic, the other by Enigma. Participants were able to identify which was which 70 per cent of the time in this test. How about you?

**REALM:** Royal, male, astray in kingdom (5)
Ground and cooked meal following recipe (5)

**SURE:** Convinced potential user (4)
User out, convinced (4)

**SEWER:** Second vessel becomes a drain (5)
Drain fresh ewers (5)

**SOLID:** Betrayed but holding one to be sound (5)
Firm penny after essential oils (5)

**TILLER:** Excited trill around note to key (6)
Territory inherited by sick, arable farmer (6)

# Arcane

*Grids, themes, gimmicks and other constraints*
*setters place on themselves*

The entirety of the English language is available to the
setter – until, that is, the moment he or she chooses a grid.

The grid determines the lengths of the answers, but
that's just for starters.

A British cryptic has 15 squares in each row and
column. That gives 53,919,893,334,301,279,589,334,030,174,03
9,261,347,274,288,845,081,144,962,207,220,498,432 ways of
arranging those 225 black and white cells – but very few of
them would make a decent puzzle, or have a pleasing look.
With a quick crossword, it's thirteen, which is still
knocking on for seven and a half sedecillion combinations.
British crosswords are symmetrical: all of them would
look the same if you rotated them through a half-circle

and, in some prettier cases, the same goes for a quarter-circle turn. There are usually between twenty-eight and thirty-two answers, very often thirty.

Different papers make different grids available to their setters; each paper's set is chosen and refined by the puzzle editor, whose overriding criterion is fairness to the solver. In each of the *Times'* seventy-one grids, for example, at least half the letters in each answer cross with some other answer. Those letters that are 'unchecked' – that is, the ones which cross with no others – never come along more than two at a time within any answer, and where they do come in a pair, it is never at the beginning or the end of an answer. It's easier to summon a word from the back of your mind if you have a sense of how it begins. In other papers, and around the world, the details vary, but the effect is the same: to make the setter's life trickier and the solver's more enjoyable and their goal more achievable.

American grids typically have far fewer black squares, which means that it is possible to find an answer solely by filling in the entries that cross with it. Another effect is on the make-up of the words which tend to fit. Vowels make up less than two fifths of the letters in the written version of English, but about half of the letters in the American crossword version. Words such as **SPENDTHRIFT**, **WRISTWATCH** and **SWORDSMANSHIP** have many delightful characteristics, but fitting nicely into a big white grid and allowing other words to intersect with them are not among them.

All of these constraints are there before the first word goes in. As soon as that happens, the working lexicon

shrinks again, and again with the second word, and so on
... And as if these constraints were not enough, setters –
especially the more experienced – have a habit of heaping
more hindrances and demands on themselves.

Take themes. A neat example is the **PARTS OF SPEECH**
puzzle set by Daniel A. Finan for the *Los Angeles Times*.
Finan decided it would be fun to use that phrase to
construct a puzzle, reinterpreting it as 'parts of **SPEECH**'
– **SPE, PEE, EEC** and **ECH** – as portrayed by four
symmetrically placed themed answers beginning with
those letter triples. **EEC** is not the most promising start to
a word, but the poet **EE CUMMINGS** is ever available. The
criteria adopted so far set the length of the themed entries
at ten letters, and once **SPELLING BEE, PEEPING TOM** and
**ECHO CHAMBER** were placed in the grid, with **PARTS OF
SPEECH** itself across the middle, there's not a lot of room
for choice in the rest of the answers. The puzzle works
beautifully, though, because of and not in spite of the
self-imposed constraint.

Other setters use the alphabet to shackle themselves.
From time to time, a writer, usually French, will decide to
compose a poem or novel in which the language is
determined by some arbitrary and avant-garde device:
take the lipogram, where a single letter is omitted from
the entire text, as employed by Georges Perec (his book
*La Disparition* is a whodunit which contains many 'A's, 'I's,
'O's and 'U's and consonants from B fully through to Z
but not a solitary inclusion of what follows D and is apt to
forgo F). Or take the pangram, in which every letter must
appear in a sentence or stanza. In literature, decisions like

this are taken rarely and only by the brave. In crosswords, they're pretty much an everyday occurrence.

It may seem arbitrary for a setter to decide that a grid must contain all twenty-six letters somewhere or other but, again, it is the solver that benefits – if he or she notices that this is what's happening. Pangrams are rarely announced explicitly but the solver can sniff them: just as a sentence like 'quick waxy bugs jump the frozen veldt' might raise suspicions that something alphabetically unusual is going on, so too should a puzzle which has, say, both a Q and an X among the entries.

Since those letters are unusual, there's a good chance the setter has created a pangram – which means that, somewhere or other, there's going to be a J, not to mention a Z. And if you haven't yet written in an answer containing a K, it's helpful to keep that letter in your mind for the remaining clues, remembering that it might be somewhere unexpected, like at the start of a word such as **KNAVE**, **KVETCH** or **KHAKI**.

The other benefit of the apparently avant-garde is the rejuvenating effect it can have on the composition of a puzzle. A pangram (or, as some manage, the triple pangram, with at least three of every letter) restricts the options, directing the setter away from habits and repetition and towards a fresher puzzle. This is also the case when he or she decides that every answer should begin with the same letter, or every clue with the same word. Or to present the clues as rhyming couplets, as Araucaria does from time to time.

Constraints breeding creativity: not a bad description of

crosswords themselves, right down to their smallest
element: the clue. A good clue is, by and large, a terse clue.
The solver needs somewhere to start, which means that
the setter must condense wordplay, definition and letter
count into a surface reading that takes up two or three
short lines. Whatever flights of fancy and levity have
governed the fill of the grid, brevity is always to be
favoured on the level of the clue.

Brevity, that is, up to a point – as the first *Times*
crossword editor Ronald Carton insisted. A paper
shortage during the Second World War led to a request
that crossword clues be shortened. Not possible, insisted
Carton, since the clues were already written with the
greatest economy: 'That is what makes them bright and
pungent. To cut down what is already succinct is to impair
the general quality of the work.'

# An unusual book

One solver who can match any setter for discipline
is Anne R. Bradford. While pregnant in 1957, she
became hooked on the *Observer*'s puzzles and began
assembling for herself a solving aid: a list of words
used in clues and what they turned out to mean. She
has kept doing so ever since, adding what she gleans
from a further twenty or so puzzles each week.

Every so often, her lists are transferred from lever-
arch files to a book: *Bradford's Crossword Solver's
Dictionary*. *Bradford's* is a reference work that does not
resemble any other. It's not really a dictionary; neither
is it a thesaurus. 'A thesaurus is mostly synonyms,' she
explains. 'Mine isn't. Under "pan", I might have "Peter",
and under "Peter", I might have "blue".'

If there is one item that reflects the decades of allusion,
sly reference and counter-intuitive mental leaps that
crosswords have spawned, it is Anne's collection of
words. For solvers, regular dictionaries are helpful up
to a point, but Bradford's is the name they whisper
to each other when they feel like sharing their secret
weapon.

# Hone

*Do crosswords really stave off dementia?*

If you want to lend a character in a film or TV programme an intelligent air, stick a crossword in front of them. The puzzle serves as a shorthand for a vague cluster of cleverness indicators, such as impressive powers of recall, sizeable vocabulary and perhaps speedy lateral thinking.

One link between crosswords and the brain that everyone seems certain about is that they yield greater dividends the older you get: a puzzle a day keeps dementia at bay. Well, not quite 'certain', I think to myself as I wander over to the corner of an Oxford pub towards a waiting psychologist, but certainly many people know an elderly relative who does such and such a puzzle every morning and still has all his or her faculties.

In a chair near the loos, I strap on a pair of noise-reduction headphones and begin the psychological test.

Kathryn Friedlander and her colleague Philip Fine are interested in solvers' cognitive skills and motivational drivers. She has joined the weekly get-together for setters, solvers and crossword bloggers organized by husband and wife John Henderson (Enigmatist, who has been setting for the *Guardian* since he was fifteen years old) and Jane Teather (who writes about crosswords at solvers' blog *Fifteen Squared*). It's informal in every sense; John used to solve solo in pubs on Saturdays and, when he noticed that others wanted to look over his shoulder or join in, decided that a better approach than being annoyed would be actively to invite others.

John and Jane meet a different cross-section of crossworders each weekend as they travel around London and Britain; this week the crowd includes Kathryn, who wants to learn more about how solvers think. She has devised a series of exercises for three groups: solvers, expert solvers and non-crossworders. I am invited to count the number of vowels in various words, then fill in the blanks in some others. I suspect that the first task is designed to hobble me in the second by planting in my head various unhelpful linguistic shapes and sounds. The research is ongoing, but I learn something about myself, and not something flattering: while I appreciate that the point of the exercise is academic enrichment, I find that I urgently want to get a decent 'score'.

Afterwards, we chat about Kathryn's curiosity regarding whether crossword solvers are better able than most to recover from misdirection when attempting tasks which

demand pattern-matching and creative association. The
tasks have been designed to give her a sense of what's
happening in the brain when it is led to a misleading place
then recovers its bearings and enjoys what the crossword
world calls the 'penny-drop' moment of clarity. For me, at
least, I tell her, there's an addictive quality to the
experience of letting go of the apparent meaning of a clue
and seeing the message hidden in code that leads to the
real interpretation.

We discuss a paper with the title 'Eye-Witnesses
Should Not Do Cryptic Crosswords Prior to Identity
Parades' from the journal *Perception*, which concludes that
solving a cryptic has a detrimental effect on subsequent
face recognition, and that the same does not go for quick
crosswords, reading or sudoku. It's a convincing piece of
research which presents its results cleanly and without
undue speculation as to the reasons behind them. I ask
Kathryn whether she has come across any similarly decent
investigations into whether crosswords are good for older
people's minds. There's not much in the papers, in the
sense of peer-reviewed journals, but there's plenty in the
other sort of papers: headlines such as the *Daily Mail*'s
**FORGET POPPING PILLS – THE BEST WAY TO BOOST YOUR
BRAINPOWER IS A CROSSWORD OR SUDOKU.**

It's from the newspapers that people I know – relatives
and co-workers – have got the idea that crosswords are a
prophylactic against Alzheimer's. Newspapers are of
course also the place where crosswords (and now sudokus)
are most readily available, so the association is presumably
good for circulation.

There are more such articles every couple of months, and if the combined reports are to be believed, here's the truth about crosswords: solving is a handy way of hanging on to your faculties, but this comes at a cost. And the price is paid by your waistline. In 2009 there was a slurry of stories warning that solving puzzles makes you fat, all citing research by Dr Kathleen Martin Ginis into whether exercising willpower in one activity leaves less resolve when you approach others.

Since solving is often a seated pastime, it's not difficult to visualize a connection between crosswords and gastric girth – and the same goes for the idea that crosswords are a kind of brain-saving mental workout. You can see vividly how both claims might be true. Alternatively, they might both be false. Or they might be neither, in the sense that nobody has actually tested either.

In the case of the crossword obesity epidemic, it's the last of those options. Ginis's research didn't include any sudokus or crosswords. 'Someone told me that the story had been in the UK press,' she told the BBC. 'I was quite excited. I googled it, I saw it and I just cringed. I felt sick.'

Probe too deeply into the evidence for stories which use words such as **NEUROBICS** and **BRAINERCISE**, and you'll find yourself similarly baffled and confounded. Here's the clearest statement I've seen about the facts of the matter, at least for American puzzles. It's from a paper called 'Predictors of Crossword Puzzle Proficiency and Moderators of Age-Cognition Relations', and it is, to say the least, deflating: 'The results provide no evidence to suggest that amount of crossword puzzle experience

reduces age-related decreases in fluid cognition or
enhances age-related increases in crystallized cognition.'
In other words, solve if you like, but don't think it will stop
you going gaga.

Kathryn's experience is similar. Crosswords may or may
not have these beneficial effects but the evidence isn't
there to tell us much. Besides, she adds, what aspects of
which kind of crossword are we talking about?

Some elements of solving (retaining pieces of vocabulary
[SEE 28 ACROSS], for example, and acronyms) tend to
improve with age, while others (preserving ambiguities,
switching from the big picture to the details) decline.
A proper examination of popular computer games
with names such as *Professor Okinaga's Cerebral Zumba*
revealed that users are no better at memory, concentration,
planning or problem-solving than non-users; what these
programmes do is make you good at the next volume
you buy of *Professor Okinaga's Cerebral Zumba*, and there's
no reason to believe that the same is not the case
with crosswords.

And what of the real-world anecdotal examples: the
avidly solving relatives who have retained their marbles?
Can we say with any certainty whether the solving is the
cause of the retention of marbles, or the retention of
marbles the cause of the solving, or whether both share an
earlier cause? Crucially, I'd like to know more about
whether this relative solves alone or with a friend or
relative [SEE 21 ACROSS].

Kathryn is more open to the idea that co-solving might
have benefits for the elderly, and she is not alone in her

interest in the social angle. I'd recommend crosswords over sudokus as a morning activity in the Rusty Cogs Retirement Home on the basis that you're less likely to call out an interesting sudoku column for everyone to enjoy or to find yourself inspired to relate an anecdote on the basis of an especially amusing '7' in that day's grid. Whatever puzzle you choose, a daily challenge that offers temporary goals and some pleasure is not a bad thing; as a cheap way of dealing with mental-health problems in an ageing population, however, it may not be enough.

The image of crosswords as intrinsic Alzheimer-bashers seems unlikely to go away any time soon. For one thing, there's the legacy of the notion that you have to be particularly intelligent to solve a broadsheet cryptic – a relic from the days when the *Times* crossword was an establishment emblem [SEE 9 ACROSS]. This is not shared by everyone: Adrian Bell, the first *Times* setter [SEE 17 DOWN], told a suitor of his daughter who had expressed admiration for his craft that crosswords were 'a complete waste of time, dear boy'.

For another, the association has a distinct appeal for setters and solvers, both of whom are often asked to explain why on earth they channel their time and energy into puzzles. 'Still, it staves off dementia, I suppose' lets them off the hook. But the implicit charge – that crosswords are a waste of time – is not one that needs to be countered. There's no real comfort in seeing the newspapers which decried the arrival of the crossword in the twenties and proscribed their use on grim utilitarian grounds [SEE 26 ACROSS] now prescribing their use on a similarly dispiriting cost/benefit basis.

And so I leave Kathryn to her research and look back across the pub to the gathered solvers, all of whom are there because it's a congenial way to spend an afternoon and an opportunity to have a stiff word or two with the setters of some recent troublesome clues. That's an end in itself. If you want to do a puzzle, you don't need a doctor's note.

# Caveat emptor

And for every bold claim ...

> **DOING A CROSSWORD DAILY CAN
> HELP PREVENT DEMENTIA**
>
> *– Mirror*, 1 December 2011

... there is a bold counter-claim ...

> **THIS PUZZLE IS DRIVING ME BARMY;
> BRAIN WORK 'SPEEDS DEMENTIA'**
>
> *– Mirror*, 2 September 2010

For every piece of advice ...

> **FOR PRESERVING OUR BRAIN POWER,
> PUZZLES BEAT VITAMINS OR
> WORKOUTS, SAY SCIENTISTS**
>
> *–Daily Mail*, 27 April 2013

... there is a caveat.

> **DITCH THAT CROSSWORD AND
> TAKE A WALK IF YOU WANT TO
> BEAT DEMENTIA**
>
> *–Daily Mail*, 22 October 2012

# Racy

*The many ways of being rude in a crossword*

In the 'Men of Letters' episode of *Steptoe and Son*, the hapless Harold gets his break as a journalist when he writes a piece for the church magazine. Sadly, the same issue contains a crossword set by his incorrigible father, Albert, which results in all copies being confiscated by the police and destroyed:

> HAROLD: Filth, filth, filth! Right the way through, from 1 across to 38 down. A concentrated square of obscenity, of filth and hardcore pornography ... Three old ladies had to be treated for shock down the Derby and Joan.

> ALBERT: Well if they didn't know the words, how could they fill 'em in?

Rarely is a crossword entry ruder than its successful solver, though that doesn't stop the setters from trying. The British setters, that is. American puzzles maintain an air of respectability and so eschew clues that fail the 'Sunday-morning-breakfast test'. When Denise Sutherland's book *Solving Cryptic Crosswords for Dummies* was being prepared for the American market, the relatively innocuous clues 'Five engaged in awkward caresses lead to rifts (9)' and 'Jenny and I go, mischievously loving (8)' were changed to 'Eve's ugly scars cause rifts (9)' and 'Appreciating Jenny, I go nuts (8)'. The setter Donk chose the *mot juste* in his clue 'He is one that could be embarrassing for American (3)', which gives a cryptic definition via the chemical symbol He and a straight borborygmic definition of **GAS**.

British crossworders, by contrast, take all of the English language as their working vocabulary, even – and for some setters, especially – the naughty bits. Any potential embarrassment or apparent smuttiness adds to the fun.

Not that you have to have a rude answer for a clue to be blue. The language of wordplay can be suggestive, even though the setter may with a straightish face insist that any lewdness is all in the solver's mind. 'Topless', say, merely means that the first letter of some word or other needs to be removed in a down clue, like in this apparent evocation of Manet's *Déjeuner sur l'herbe* from the *Telegraph* ...

**Relaxed when lying in grass (topless) (5)**

... which is merely asking you to remove the 'top' letter of 'reed' and insert 'as' for 'when' to make **EASED**. Likewise, 'movement' is a standard indicator of an anagram, so even when the *Guardian*'s Bonxie asks you to consider a 'bowel movement'...

**Push out bowel movement (5)**

... he is merely seeing whether the solver is able to tell that general area of the body from his or her **ELBOW**. Definitions can themselves evoke imagery loucher than the answer: in crosswordese, a 'Swingers' bar' may be simply a **TRAPEZE**.

John Halpern, who sets as Paul, Mudd, Punk and Dada, is one of the rudest setters currently working. He sets for all the broadsheets, which vary in the scope they give him for salaciousness. Of his tendency towards the bawdy, he writes:

> [T]he art of creating a cryptic crossword so lends itself to these things. The indicators we use to suggest the type of clue include 'insertions' and 'penetrations' (of and by words) and the reversal (or taking from behind) of ideas. Then there are anagram indicators. Any synonym of 'drunk', 'mad' or 'messed up' may be employed – and the less puritan of you may be able to think of some naughty examples.

The reverse is also true of course: the clues which trip you up with a dirty answer to a clean surface, such as the *Times* Jumbo's 'I'll be doing a quick exposure (with a flash) (8)' for **STREAKER**, Anax's 'It's getting away (5, 7)' for **DIRTY WEEKEND** and Nimrod's 'Crack construction worker shows up on site (8, 6)' for **BUILDER'S BOTTOM**.

The next ring of our inferno of rudeness is the sweary

clue. These come in two types. In the first, the swear word is not uttered explicitly but needs to be part of the solver's vocabulary if the wordplay is to yield.

When Monk says 'Bang up following nonsense after one's dismissal (5)', you need to remove an I (one) from a synonym for 'nonsense' before adding an 'up' for SHTUP. And that from the *Financial Times* – the paper whose crossword is 'pink and hard in the morning', as the old gag has it. And in the most difficult crosswords – the weekend ones without any black squares – all language is fair game.

The erudite *Listener*, the themes of which have included particle physics and Biblical errata [SEE 10 ACROSS], is open-ended enough in its subject matter to have included in the puzzle by Alban titled 'Brassless Load' the bawdy rhyme ''Twas Christmas Day in the Workhouse'. The title is the anagram of the three words that rhyme with 'walls', 'Gods' and 'brass' in the filthy seasonal ditty, which, as the puzzle's preamble states, can be found in *Brewer's Dictionary of Phrase and Fable*. In another, 'Fundamentally Flawed' by Monk, the theme 'bottoms up' was reflected by asking solvers to invert in the down entries CHEROOT, PANIC BUTTON, BUMS ON SEATS, SCRUMPTIOUS, FOREARM and NEW YEAR'S EVE the hidden synonyms for the buttocks. In 2006, the *Listener*'s venerable crossword cousin, Azed [SEE 13 DOWN], offered the clue 'Teetotaller worried re "dirt" imbibed by worthless fellow (12, hyphenated)' for WATER-DRINKER. Azed himself wrote in his Azed slip that accompanies each puzzle:

The reference to 'wanker' in my clue to **WATER-DRINKER** raised a few eyebrows, though I hardly paused before deciding to use it, regarding Azed solvers as a broad-minded lot and considering it relatively mild as coarse expressions go these days.

He's right, in that, since then, we've seen in the broadsheets the second type of sweary clue, where the cuss word is not merely in the solver's mind but printed in black and white, or black and pink in the example of 'Fat cats in shit – excellent! (9)' for **FANTASTIC**, also from Monk in the *FT*.

Sometimes, the expletive in question is less rude in context, for instance Paul's 'Fresh velvety cut or laminated edges for the buggers? (4, 2, 3, 5)', which was published during the phone-hacking scandal for the **NEWS OF THE WORLD** (new+soft+hew+or+LD). But in clues like Arachne's ...

**Throw shoe! Bugger invaded Iraq! (6, 4)**

... for **GEORGE BUSH**, it's justified only by the topical allusion to Muntadar al-Zaidi's 2008 footwear attack on the president and by the smile on the solver's face.

That mixture of the political and the potty-mouthed is the trademark of another crossword institution. The line that's occasionally crossed by Fleet Street is jumped over and left gasping in the muck by the puzzle in *Private Eye*.

The *Eye* puzzle is the one which best combines a British affection for dirty words with erudition and wordplay. Its first setter was Tiresias, better known as the MP and security-service asset Tom Driberg. The magazine's official history describes his stint from 1969 until 1976 as 'legendarily filthy'. Driberg had been receiving a retainer for providing parliamentary gossip; when this dried up because he was not in the Commons often enough to pick up much intelligence, he suggested that he instead set a prize crossword.

Driberg was unusual among setters in that he would arrive at the offices of his publisher and dictate clues in person rather than sending a puzzle in the post. In his official history of *Private Eye*, Adam MacQueen explains that the incorrigible Driberg did so as a pretext for flirting with and ogling members of the staff.

As Tiresias – a pseudonym taken from the blind transsexual son of the nymph Chariclo – he seemed intent on using the most graphic imagery possible while retaining cryptic integrity. Driberg's biographer, Francis Wheen, declares his finest moment in setting to be crossword 98, from 1972. This included the clues 'Seamen mop up anal infusions (6)' and 'Sounds as if you must look behind for this personal lubricant (5)'; it was a prize puzzle and the £2 went to one Mrs Rosalind Runcie, whose husband was then the Bishop of St Albans and went on to become Archbishop of Canterbury.

The Tiresias tradition is maintained by the current setter Cyclops:

**Very Boris to go topless and shake knightly equipment? (5)**

**Welcome Bill Clinton's first two touches on excellent Monica's top (7)**

**Acceptable to have an orgasm? Top bankers want theirs much-enhanced (6)**

Answers in the Notes ...

The joy of a Cyclops clue is that the relentless smut seems to place even more onus on the wordplay to stand up; the puzzles are also charmingly erudite, witty and well informed about current affairs – especially when they involve current politicians having affairs. Tiresias and Cyclops are positively prudish, though, in comparison to the rudest setter in the game.

Given the imagery in some of its cartoons and the eye-watering vocabulary in its Profanisaurus collection of rude words, it is saying something to note that the crossword is the most obscene page in *Viz* comic. Reading through the clues by setter Anus is like peering at the cubicle-wall scribblings of a gleefully verbose sociopath, and there is a kind of magic in seeing each filthy rant resolve to a perfectly structured combination of wordplay and definition in *Viz*'s standard, symmetrical grids. Publications reflect their ethos in their crosswords, and *Viz*'s is the *sine qua non* – an erudite visionary intellect, Anus sets for all the broadsheets – channelled into the pure purpose of unstinting, startling smut.

From **AARD-ON** to **ZZ BOTTOM**, they are, after all, only words. And to finish with perhaps setters' favourite 'perfectly innocent' double meaning, if the clue 'In which three couples get together for sex (5)' from a *Times* Crossword Championship puzzle makes you think of anything other than the **LATIN** for 'six', that's your problem.

HAROLD: I've just got three things to say to you. 6 across, 13 across and 28 down.

ALBERT: (checking puzzle) Don't you dare use language like that to me!

HAROLD: Up your 14 across!

# Blue clues?

The sneakiest kind of blue clue is one where the entire surface meaning is suggestive of something suggestive, but the answer is something you'd be happy to say over breakfast in the seventies with a bishop's wife. Here are ten examples, with two down clues at the bottom:

Delicately conceal daughter, naked, greeting current boyfriend (4, 1, 4, 4)

Puff of vapour emanating from women behind (4)

One adopting missionary position? (10)

Panties do chafe down under (9)

Aussie singer's extremely kinky romance? (5)

One is not going all the way, chasing better cock (5)

Erotic pose one ignored on page three, say (5)

Love god seen at horny beast's rear? (4)

Leggy stripper fails to keep bottom in position (5)

Caught girl in her underwear under a bit of a spell? (11)

# Solutions

# Solutions

The answers to the clues mentioned in the chapters are as follows:

**PLUM:** The answer to 'Exclaim when the twine gives out' is the musical instruction **STRINGENDO**; it is a clue that is hard to love.

**RAILWAYMEN:** Across: 1 **HAT**, 6 **BEDDERS**, 8 **GI**, 9 **USE**, 10 **CHAS**, 11 **SCREAM**, 12 **SAW**, 15 **BARSO**, 17 **CHRISSY BOY**, 19 **SOS**, 20 **EEL**; Down: 1 **ALIBI**, 5 **SEVEN**, 7 **SUGGS**, 8 **HEART**, 10 **CAR**, 13 **WOODY**, 14 **PONY**, 15 **BIRDS**, 16 **ACES**, 18 **ONE**."

**STRONG:**

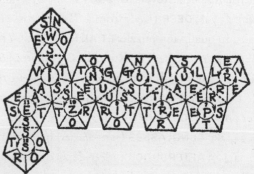

BEGINNER: Double definitions: **LAUNCH** (a noun and then a verb) by Virgilius in *Sunday Telegraph* 2,596; **LOCO** (adjective, then noun) and **NAIL-BITING** (adjective, then noun) by Paul, the latter in *Guardian* 25,097. **PASS** (verb, noun, verb) from *Times* 24,989; **BUTT** (noun, noun, verb, noun) by Nestor in *Independent* 8,181; **KNOCK OFF** (verb, verb, verb, verb, adjective) from *Times* Jumbo 830. **Cryptic definitions: BEAR IN MIND** by Orlando in *Guardian* Quiptic 577; **OVER THE HILL** from *Times* Jumbo 998; **BOTTOMLESS** from *Times* 24,611. **FISHMONGER** by Mudd in *FT* 13,512; **BIGAMIST** from *Telegraph* 25,865; **MATADORS** from *Sunday Telegraph* 2,631. **Anagrams: OVERSIGHT** (*giveshort*) by Dac in *Independent* 8,145; **OUTLANDISH** (*ishouldtan*) by Puck in *Guardian* 25,742; **INSISTENCE** (*scenesinit*) by Mudd in *FT* 13,494. **OLD MASTER** (*artsmodel*) from *Times* 24,610; **TRAINSPOTTERS** (*transportsite*) by Boatman in *Guardian* 24,556; **CONIFER** (*fircone*) from *Telegraph* 27,103. **Hidden answers: BREACH OF PROMISE** from *Times* Jumbo 744; **LECH** by Puck in *Guardian* 25,445; **HIDDEN** by Brian Greer in *Sunday Telegraph* 2,607. **RIDER** by Dac in *Independent* 7,791; **ROTISSERIE** from *Sunday Telegraph* 2,590; **DEMI MOORE** by Osmosis in *Telegraph* Toughie 636. **Reversals: SNOT** (*tons*) by Tramp in *Guardian* 25,798; **DEER** (*reed*) from a *Times* Crossword Championship qualifying puzzle; **ET AL** (*late*) from *Times* 25,015; **PISA** (*a+sip* reversed) by Rufus in *Guardian* 25,659; **AWARD** (*draw+a* reversed) from *Sunday Telegraph* 2,676; **OMEGA** (*o* then *a+gem* reversed) from *Times* 24,876. **One thing after another: CAST-OFF** (*cast+off*) by Orlando in *Guardian* 24,489; **SUNGLASSES** (*sung+lasses*) by Paul in *Guardian* 24,407; **AFTERSHOCK** (*afters+hock*) by Chifonie in *Guardian* 24,525. **CLEFT** (*C+left*) by Gordius in *Guardian* 24,537; **TRICEPS** (*trice+PS*) by Philistine in *Guardian* 25,684; **CEREBRAL** (*c+ere+bra+L*) by Warbler in *Telegraph* Toughie 938. **Soundalikes**: **SUITE** (*sweet*) by Chifonie in *Guardian* 25,482; **NEIGH** (*nay*) by Cincinnus in *FT* 13,670; **COKES** (*coax*) from *Sunday Times* 4,269. **MOOSE** (*mouse*) by Araucaria in *Guardian* 25,492; **EYEBROW** (*highbrow*) by Crucible in *Guardian* 24,379; **ANOINTS** (*an ounce*) by Tramp in *Guardian* 25,471. Acrostics: **BAWL** by Orlando in *Guardian* 25,513; **IMAM** by Bunthorne in *Guardian* 23,570; **NEAT** by Viking in *FT* 13,308. **GATEAU** (*a tea* in *GU*) by Nimrod in *Inquisitor* 1,221; **ANTI-WAR** (*TI* in *Anwar*) by Kruger, extracted from a more fiendish clue in *Enigmatic Variations* 1,052; **TWO-TIMED** (*Tim* in *woe* in *TD*) by Phi in *Independent* 8,182. **All-in-ones**: **NINJA** (hidden answer) by Mudd in *FT* 14,233; **YES MAN** (anagram of *naysme*) by Quixote in *Independent on Sunday* 1,071; **VOLCANO** (anagram of *ovalcone* minus *E*) by Redshank in *FT* 14,030; **TRIPE** (middle letter of *shorthorn* + *ripe*) by Styx in *FT* 14,059; **PATISSERIE** (anagram of *itspiesare*) from *Sunday Telegraph* 2,609; **TABLE FOR TWO** (anagram of first letters of *romantics want* with *abottleof*) by Enigmatist in *Guardian* 24,325; **OAKEN** (anagram of *one* around *a* and *K*) by Taupi in *Guardian* 24,116; **MARIE ANTOINETTE** (anagram of *atonetimearentI*) by Paul in *Guardian* 25,481; **APOSTROPHE** (anagram of *perhapstoo*) by Rufus in *Telegraph* 25,985; **DING DONG DELL PUSSY'S IN THE WELL** (anagram of *downplightneedlessbullyings*) by Pasquale in *Guardian* 25,776. **EVENTS** The across answers to the **telekinesis puzzle** are **ERDA** and **EYED**. The **answers to the seasonal clues** are **BURNS NIGHT** by Pasquale in *Guardian* 25,844; **SHROVE TUESDAY** by Pasquale in *Guardian* 25,403; **MOTHERING SUNDAY** by Araucaria in *Guardian* 24,851; **ALL FOOLS' DAY** by Virgilius in *Sunday Telegraph* 2,633; **MAYDAY** from *Sunday Telegraph* 2,480; **SUMMER SOLSTICE** from *Sunday Telegraph* 2,551; **HENLEY REGATTA** from *Times* 25,135; **LAMMAS** from *Times* 24,062; **AUTUMNAL EQUINOX** by Glow-worm in *Independent on Sunday* 1144; **HALLOWE'EN** from *Times* 24,916; **BONFIRE NIGHT** by Jeremy Mutch in *Telegraph* 26,078; **HOGMANAY** from *Sunday Times* 4,205.

**WING**: Sarah Hayes' three topical clues are **IMPRISON** from *Guardian* 25,390, **TONY BLAIR** from *Guardian* 25,057 (both as Arachne) and **NEWS OF THE WORLD** from *Independent* 7,975 (as Anarche).

**IBEX**: The answers to the new chestnuts are: **ORCHESTRA** by Dante in *FT* 14,081; **STRESSED** by Crux in *FT* 14,111; **MANCHESTER CITY** by Orlando in *Guardian* 24,199; **AUBERGINE** by Armonie in *FT* 14,240; **LEGEND** by Elkamere in *Telegraph* Toughie 921.

**ALL THE SAME?**: **ANAESTHETIST** by Rover in *Guardian* 24,574 (someone who makes you numb might be a 'number'); **CLUB** by Brummie in *Guardian* 25,795 ('clubs' has had its tail removed or been 'de-tailed'); **NON-ACADEMIC** by Dean Mayer in *Sunday Times* 4,479 ('supply' working as an adverb); **CANDLESTICKS** from *Telegraph* 26,182 (candles have wicks and so are perhaps 'wicked things'); **UNRAVEL** by Cincinnus from *FT* 13,554 (in the town of Nancy, 'one' is said 'un'); **DE-ICER** from Donk in *Independent on Sunday* 1,200 (one doe is a deer, two does are some deer).

**ORIGIN**: *See top of facing page.*

**NINA:** The *Telegraph* **Quick puns** are Sherlock Holmes, Marcel Proust, Chattanooga, Whitney Houston, Berlioz, Damascus, Tutankhamun, Tanzania, Buster Keaton, Basil Fawlty, Picasso, Evelyn Waugh, Roxy Music, Bill Clinton, Bucharest, Amadeus, Cervantes, Australia, Hey Jude and Bruce Willis.

**BYGONE:** The answer to the **inaugural double acrostic** is also given in verse, with **HAWAII** rendered jocosely as **O-WHY-HEE:**

**The Words**

**LONDON**'s the 'world in little'; 'make a note on't.'

**THAMES** is its cesspool; that's the long and short on't.

**The Letters**

At State receptions in day's untaxed *Light*,

Are *Ostrich* plumes a fair and goodly sight.

The *Neva* with old Thames will ne-ver cope,

Though *Despotism* dwell in Naples soap.

As for poor Cook, *O-why-hee* must excuse

The tale of his sad fate; 'tis now no *News*.

**RULED:** The answers to the **Azed competition clues** are **MAGIC LANTERN** by N. C. Dexter for Azed 1,648; **BODY-SNATCHER**

by C. J. Morse for Azed 482; **BRAINWASH** by L. May for Azed 92. The answers to the Crosaire clues are **LITERAL**; **RATHER**; **ASPIRATES**; **LEGISLATE**; **LEVERET**; **HAS**; **STENCH**; **OFT**; **STARTS**; **BUTTER**; **EVEREST**; **SWORD-PLAY**.

**TONGUE-TIED**: Torquemada's answers are **LIGHT SWITCH** (via slight witch), **WELSH HARP** (harsh whelp) and **THE YEOMEN OF THE GUARD** (the go-men of the Yard). The answers to the spoonergram are **TINY WAIST** and **WINY TASTE**. The *New York Times* answers are from 20 June 2012: **BUSTER KEATON** (Custer beaten), **JAMES TAYLOR** (tames jailer) and the man who complained about not featuring in crosswords [SEE 8 ACROSS], **NORMAN MAILER** (Mormon nailer). The answers to the 10 cryptic clues are: **NIGHTLIFE** by Anax in *Independent* 8,056; **TOODLE-PIP** by Qaos in *Guardian* 25,530; **PACKED LUNCH** by Pasquale in *Guardian* 25,810; **FLAT CAP** by Araucaria in *Guardian* 25,266; **BEAN CURD** from *Telegraph* 26,719; **SEA BREEZE** by Enigmatist in *Guardian* 25,000; **HATE MAIL** by Hamilton in *FT* 13,911; **BUTTERFLY** by Don Manley in *Chambers Crossword Manual*; **FLAT BATTERY** by Paul in *Guardian* 25,065; **GIFT WRAP** by David Astle in *Sydney Morning Herald*, 23 March 2010.

**SETTLERS**: Torquemada: **OBADIAH**; Adrian Bell: **SWISS ROLL**, **ICE CUBE** and **MARS**; Ximenes: **ESTUARY** and **OSLO**.

**WHODUNIT**: The answer to Dexter's clue is **OBLITERATE**, the winning entry in Ximenes' 945th clueing competition (1967). The **hidden names** in the *Times* puzzle, reprinted in *75 Years of the Times Crossword*, are **BARRINGTON PHELOUNG**, **JOHN THAW** and **COLIN DEXTER**. Superstates: **ABACUS** by Edward Karasek, **USA** Today 20 April 2005; **ROAD RAGE** by Nina Rulon-Miller, *Chronicle of Higher Education*, 4 June 2010; **DNA**

by John Lampkin, *Los Angeles Times*, 5 September 2010; **KISS ME** by Mark Milhet & Rich Norris, *Los Angeles Times*, 2 June 2007; **HELLO** by Myles Callum, *Wall Street Journal*, 6 November 2009; **ART** by Leonard Williams, *USA Today*, 30 May 2006; **PREGNANT** by Tracy Gray, *New York Times*, 14 June 2012; **RADAR TRAPS** by Doug Peterson, *Newsday*, 26 December 2009; **FIG LEAF** by Barry C Silk, *Newsday*, 24 July 2010 and **LOO** by Barry C Silk, *Newsday*, 24 July 2010.

**ENIGMA:** The answer to the '*Telegraph* Six' **Rufus clue** is **CLIMBDOWN**. The **Enigma** clues are 'Ground and cooked meal following recipe', 'Convinced potential user', 'Drain fresh ewers', 'Firm penny after essential oils' and 'Excited trill around note to key'.

**RACY:** The answers to the **bowdlerized Dummies** clues are **CREVASSES** and **ENJOYING**; Denise lists nine other inappropriate clues in her post 'The Rude Clues' at the *alwayspuzzling.blogspot.com.au* blog. The answers to the **Tiresias** clues are **ENEMAS** and **SEBUM** and **Cyclops's** answers are **VISOR** from *Private Eye* 484, **ACCLAIM** from 487 and **INCOME** from 483; Cyclops also contributes much less salacious clues for the *Guardian* as Brummie. The **answers to the blue clues** are: **DRAW A VEIL OVER** from *Times* 25,015; **WAFT** by Nimrod in *Independent* 7,816; **EVANGELIST** by Ray Terrell in *Telegraph* 26,908; **ANTIPODES** by Firefly in *Telegraph* Toughie 848; **KYLIE** by Dac in *Independent* 8,025; **CAPON** by Anax in *Independent* 7,998; **RECTO** by Orlando in *Guardian* 25,607; **EROS** by Dada in *Telegraph* Toughie 914; **LOCUS** and **ABRACADABRA** from the same smutty puzzle, *Times* 25,147.

# Notes

**PLUM:** Wodehouse's **grandson** spoke to Simon Hoggart in the *Guardian* piece 'Farewell to our Man in Caracas', 1 November 2008. The crossword-using **pastor** was the Reverend George McElveen and the quotation is from Wodehouse's memoir *Bring on the Girls*. The **queen's morning routine** is described in a 1992 *Vanity Fair* profile and **Sepp Blatter**'s reading matter in the CNN profile 'Sepp Blatter Revealed'. **Ian McCulloch** was talking to *Uncut* in July 1998 and the **Indira Gandhi** story is related as part of the British Diplomatic Oral History Programme.

**RAILWAYMEN:** In **Morse**'s crossword, one of the clues – 'Bradman's famous duck (6)', for which the answer is **DONALD** – is attributed to a setter called Quixote; in real life, the setter Quixote is Don Manley, the author of *The Chambers Crossword Manual*. In the manual, Manley explains why the clue is, in his words, extremely elegant, but also brilliant, citing Don Bradman's notorious dismissal at the

Oval in 1948 and adding, 'Oh, that I *had* written it!' The
**Barming-to-Swanley** letter was sent by Fran Williams in
2003 and is reprinted in *75 Years of the Times Crossword*, and
the team-spirit letter is reprinted in '*Times* Puzzle isn't for
the Faint of Brain' in the *Montreal Gazette*, 27 May 1978.
The crack writing team for **Beryl Reid** *Says Good Evening*
included N. F. Simpson, John Mortimer and Harold Pinter;
POLYHYMNIA raises an extra smile for seasoned solvers
because of the more frequent appearances of the muse ERATO
in puzzles [SEE 28 ACROSS]. 'Clues and answers should not
be discussed in public' is reprinted in Roger Millington's
*Crossword Puzzles: Their History and Their Cult*, along with a
correspondent who describes how the speedier solvers hold
up a puzzle completed in ink 'hoping that those poor fish are
marvelling at our superiority and are surreptitiously trying
to cheat'. The change in **carriage design** and other aspects
of the commute are described in Joe Moran's *Queuing for
Beginners: The Story of Daily Life from Breakfast to Bedtime*.
The clue in '**Cardiac Arrest**' has an unconventional form: we
know the answer is of seven letters, begins and ends with C,
and is similar to the name of an American automobile, which
the video suggests is a Cadillac. **Anthony Grey**'s experience
is described in his memoir *Hostage in Peking* and the clues
he wrote in captivity can be found in the puzzle collections
*Crosswords From Peking* and *Chinese Puzzles*. The NOSE/ROSE
confusion in the *Two Ronnies* sketch is in series eight and
was also exploited by the real-life Puck in *Guardian* 25,594
with his clue 'Scents of flowers newly opened (5)' for NOSES.
THAILAND is from *The Smoking Room* series two, episode
eight and BONTEMPI from series two, episode seven. The

**National Inquirer** clues are from the *Cheers* episode 'Coach in Love Part 2', and **Victor Meldrew** battles with the cryptic in the episode 'The Trial'.

**STRONG**: Stephen **Sondheim** was talking to Norman Lebrecht for the piece 'A Funny Thing Happened to Stephen Sondheim' in *La Scena Musicale*, 14 July 2004. The *Listener* **parody** is in *Not! The Nine O'Clock News* by Sean Hardie and John Lloyd. The *Listener* magazine ceased publication in 1991 and was briefly revived by BBC News Online in 2000. The **origami** puzzle is Rentokil by Jago, the **advent calendar** Great Expectations by Samuel and the **snowflake** In Season by Lavatch. A Scientific Crossword is *Listener* 2, A Botanical Crossword is 8, A Latin Crossword is 6 and An Indian Crossword is 3. The **puzzles in the list** are Duet for One by Bandmaster, X by Pilcrow, Admission by Kea, 27 by Mango, A1 by Ifor, In Clue Order, On and On by Loda, Breach of Contract by Ron, A Double Harness: All the Queen's Horses by Leiruza, Sine Qua Non by Shackleton, Sum by Hotspur, Variation on a Theme by Nibor, Carte Très Blanche by Elgin and Carte Blanche with a Twist by Mash. Peter Robinson's **early-day motion** was tabled on 10 July 1997.

**AFFRONTS**: The 'wooden leg' complaint is related by Margaret Farrar in an interview for the *New Yorker*. **Bob Bartholomew**'s rueful memories are in *75 Years of the Times Crossword* and the request for an **emailed grid** by lunchtime is in Siobhan Butterworth's column as readers' editor, 4 February 2008. The **Merl Reagle** quotation is from the 2006 documentary *Wordplay* and Margaret Farrar's advice to the young Reagle is quoted in Dean Olsher's mesmerizing book *From Square One: A Meditation, with Digressions, on*

*Crosswords*. **FORT KNOX** is from *Guardian* 24,618. **GHANA/GARNER** is in *Independent* 7,125 by Morph; **WAR/WAUGH** and **SHORE/SHAW** are in *Guardian* 25,692 by Brummie and **PROSE AND KHANS** is from Matt Ginsberg's *New York Times* puzzle of Sunday 16 December 2012. The **Times advice** to setters is quoted in Don Manley's authoritative *Chambers Crossword Manual*. The 'Tory assassination' clue is mentioned in Sandy Balfour's *A Clue to Our Lives*; Balfour notes that the *Guardian* separately published the similar clue 'Clamour for Tory assassination (4, 6)', which would almost certainly not have passed muster in the *Telegraph* at any time. The **negresses/EGRESSES** clue can be found in Puzzle 5 of *Afrit's Armchair Crosswords: A Book for Leisure Moments*, which has been reprinted by Derek Harrison. **John Perkin's** advice to Araucaria is related in *A Clue to Our Lives*. The Araucaria **CANCER** puzzle is *Guardian* 25,842 and a sample of **the magazine 1 Across** can be obtained by sending a C5 SAE to 1 Across, The Old Chapel, Middleton Tyas, Richmond, North Yorkshire DL10 6PP.

**BEGINNER**: **EVEN** and **NATURE** are by Rufus in *Guardian* 25,819 and 25,377. **DOG-EAT-DOG** is from *Times* Jumbo 886. **ROMEO AND JULIET** is from *Everyman* 3,380; **ROOSEVELT** is by Notabilis in *Telegraph* Toughie 146. **GET-TOGETHER** is from *Times* Jumbo 926; **INSIGNIFICANT** is by Brian Greer in *Sunday Telegraph* 2,539. **SLAP** is by Firefly in *Telegraph* Toughie 474; **REGAL** is by Rufus in *Guardian* 25,239. **INTERN** is by Quixote in *Independent* 8,232. **WILD** is from *Sunday Telegraph* 2,583. **STIR** is by Rufus in *Guardian* 25,293.

**EVENTS**: **Jeremiah Farrell** was interviewed by Johnny Gee at *barelybad.com/xwdthemes_110596.htm* and is one of the organizers of Gathering for Gardner, the biennial celebration of recreational mathematician Martin Gardner. Will Shortz described **the ELECTED puzzle** during CNN's *Business Unusual* on 25 March 2002 and NBC's *Sunday Today* on 14 February 1999 and in Coral Amende's *Crossword Obsession: The History and Lore of the World's Most Popular Pastime*. On 9 July 2003, a *New York Times* puzzle by Patrick Merrell had at 20 across **TOUR DE FRANCE** and at 35 across '[Prediction] Lance Armstrong at the end of the 2003 20-Across': both **FOUR-TIME CHAMP** and **FIVE-TIME CHAMP** were valid entries, and the first letters of the first seven clues spelled out F-A-R-R-E-L-L, an appropriately arcane accolade. The **Archer clue** is in *Guardian* 22,103. The life of **the Old Vicarage** is described in Martin Garrett's *Cambridge: A Cultural and Literary History* and that of Jeffrey Archer in Michael Crick's *Jeffrey Archer: Stranger than Fiction*. **Araucaria's cogitation** with Scrabble tiles is recreated in Sandy Balfour's *Pretty Girl in Crimson Rose*, which also mentions a tribute clue written by a *Guardian* reader: 'Where shaken Archer's "I'm noble!" palls (1, 8, 6, 4)', for **A BELMARSH PRISON CELL.**

VALE: The data on **newspaper circulation** are from the 2012 Ofcom report 'Declining Circulation of Print Newspapers Occurs alongside Shift in Emphasis to Online Versions'. The **polling data** are from a YouGov online survey of 2,045 adults between 22 and 24 May 2013; the figures have been weighted and are representative of all GB adults (aged 18+). **Orlando**'s thoughts are from the *Guardian* piece 'Meet the Setter: Orlando', 13 September 2012. The *New Yorker*'s **Henry Hook** piece is by Burkhard Bilger, 4 March 2002. The Eric

**Westbrook** remarks are in the *Guardian*'s 'Three-Dimensional Cryptic Crosswords', 10 February 2012, and *calendarpuzzles. co.uk* is the home of the **charity calendars**. Tracy Gray's '**right turn**' puzzle was published on 14 June 2012.

**SPLIT**: The Keats line is from the posthumously published 'When I Have Fears that I May Cease to Be'.

**WING**: Octagonal puzzles can be seen in a photo feature about the **Soviet Union** in the 11 August 1941 edition of *Life* magazine, though *Telegraph* editor Val Gilbert wrote in *How to Crack the Cryptic Crossword* that 'the only place I know of that disclaimed all knowledge of the pastime was the Soviet Union.' **Nabokov**'s clues are described in Brian Boyd's *Vladimir Nabokov: The Early Years*. The **Douglas-Home** story is from Simon Hoggart's *Guardian* piece on the *New York Times* crossword compiled by an ex-president, 'Clinton's Cryptic Crossword Won't Impress', 8 May 2007. The **Heath/Straw** exchange was part of the Business of the House, 29 June 2006.

**DECEIT**: **Rebus**'s unabashed admission is in the novel *Set in Darkness*; Ian Rankin told the winter 1995 edition of crime-fiction magazine *A Shot in the Dark* that he chose his detective's name because 'a Rebus is a kind of picture puzzle popular at one time in the Merry Mac Fun Page of the ruthlessly parochial *Sunday Post* newspaper.' The **TAURUS** clue is by Hamilton in *FT* 14,283. A **COOF**, also spelled cuif, is an obscure Scottish word for a fool or a lout. The **Gielgud** anecdote is related in 'For Johnnie's a Jolly Good Fellow' in the *Evening Standard*, 14 April 1994.

**DIALOGUE**: **Mike Mussina**'s remarks are from the 2006 documentary *Wordplay*. **Prunella Scales** described the mints and puzzles in a *Times* piece headed '30 Years on from *Fawlty*

Towers', 19 October 2009. The *Boston Globe* **proposal puzzle** is described in the *Globe* piece 'Clued In', 23 September 2007.

**THRILLER:** The experiences of **Stanley Sedgewick** are related in Michael Smith's *Station X: The Codebreakers of Bletchley Park* and B. Jack Copeland's *Colossus: The First Electronic Computer*. The **need for a cool head** is from an interview conducted by Sinclair McKay and quoted in the *Telegraph* piece 'Cracking Hobby Won the Day', 26 August 2010. The **D-Day clues** are described in Anthony Hall's *Operation Overlord: D-Day Day by Day* and **Val Gilbert**'s thoughts are in the *Telegraph* piece 'D-Day Crosswords are Still a Few Clues Short of a Solution', 3 May 2004.

**COURTS:** '**The street finds its own** use **for things**' originated in William Gibson's story 'Burning Chrome'. On 24 August 1997 the *Mail on Sunday* reported an echo of the twenties: 'HUNDREDS of puzzled readers rang the Royal Botanical Gardens in Kew after one clue in last week's *Mail on Sunday* crossword left them baffled. Experts there came up with the answer **GRUGRU** to 25 across (Tropical American palm such as Acrocomia sclerocarpa).'

**UNAMERICAN:** The **Oxford remark** is from the website *World of Words*' FAQs: 'Is It True that English Has the Most Words of any Language?' Sandy **Balfour** was talking to the Radio 3 programme *Night Waves* on 13 February 2003.

**IBEX:** Noah **Veltman**'s analysis is summarized in the post 'Calculating "Crosswordiness" of Answers: How to Do It and What It Shows Us' at the *Guardian* Data Blog, 4 February 2013. The Georges **Perec** quotation is from his *Les Mots croisés, précédés de considérations de l'auteur sur l'art et la manière de croiser les mots*, translated by this author. Don

Manley's advice comes in the section 'A Filler on Fillers' in
his authoritative *Chambers Crossword Manual*. Bob Klahn's
clue is from *New York Times*, 20 September 1997; Monk's is
from *FT* 14,224; John Lampkin's is from *Los Angeles Times*, 2
January 2011; Tramp's is from *Guardian* 25,798.

**ALL THE SAME?:** The **Mad Hatter** exchange is from *Alice's
Adventures in Wonderland* and the **Humpty Dumpty** one
from *Through the Looking Glass*. **Afrit's Armchair Crosswords**
has been reprinted by Derek Harrison and *crossword.org.uk*
has details on how to obtain a copy.

**IMPOLITE: Gordius** describes the competition in the
introduction to the book *Guardian Crosswords: Gordius* and
in the interview at 'Meet the Setter: Gordius', *Guardian*, 15
November 2012. David **Cameron** used **LOL** in text-messages
to News International's Rebekah Brooks to convey 'lots of
love'; **BLIMEY** is one of many awkward colloquialisms in
Tony **Blair**'s memoir *A Journey*; Margaret **Thatcher** used the
Lancastrian **FRIT** in parliamentary questions, 19 April 1983.
Stephen Fry discussed **cocaine and crosswords** in Sky Arts'
*In Confidence*, 3 June 2011. **OMNISHAMBLES** was coined by
Tony Roche for series three, episode one of *The Thick of It*. It
was first used in the House by Andy Burnham the same year,
which made the show's creator Armando Iannucci 'queasy
and uneasy', and Nimrod's clue is from *Independent* 7,996.
**SCREEN** is from *Sunday Telegraph* 2,512 and **CLEAVE** is by
Rufus in *Guardian* 24,542.

**ORIGIN:** The **Stanley Newman** quotation is from his
*Cruciverbalism: A Crossword Fanatic's Guide to Life in the
Grid*. The **popular crossword books** are described in Peter
Schwed's *Turning the Pages: An Insider's Story of Simon &*

*Schuster 1924–1984.* The **Merl Reagle** remarks are from the 2006 documentary *Wordplay.* Wynne's comments recalling his attempt to **patent** the crossword are related in Clark Kinnaird's *Encyclopaedia of Puzzles and Pastimes* and his application for the rhombus-shaped puzzle is US patent number 1558071.

**NINA**: Brendan's **presidential** puzzle was *Guardian* 24,832. The story about the final **News of the World** crossword is in the *Guardian* piece '*News of the World* Staff Stow Parting Barbs in Final Edition's Crosswords', 11 July 2011. **Henry Hook**'s work can be found in his collection *Twisted Crosswords*, which contains the Crushword, where each cell may contain more than four letters, and the story of his rebuttal nina is told in a *New Yorker* piece called 'Meet the Marquis de Sade of the Puzzle World', March 2002. The puzzle by **Monk** is *Independent* 6,506. Jambazi's **Nina Simone** puzzle is *Independent* 8,168. Phi's **self-referential nina** is in *Independent* 8,129. The *Times* puzzle celebrating the marriage of **William and Kate** is number 24,836. The letter to the *Times* about **schoolmaster** Alfred Bately, from John D. Hart, is reprinted in *75 Years of the Times Crossword*, as is the letter from Wing Commander Peter Flippant. And the **Black Speech**-quoting puzzle is *FT* 14,242.

**SWIFTEST**: The **Roger McGough** lines are from 'Early Morning Poems' in his collection *Defying Gravity*, and the **Times Crossword Club** is at *www.crosswordclub.co.uk* and **Roy Dean** described his experience on the *Today* programme in 'a lunchtime talk to a Bromley society', published in the collection *Mainly in Fun* and **Colin Dexter**'s thoughts on the *Times* puzzle are from the foreword to *75 Years of the Times*

*Crossword* and there is much background on the **Times Crossword Championship** at *www.biddlecombe.demon.co.*uk/ *puzzles.html* and the remarks on the **Mark Goodliffe** era of that contest are from contemporary news reports and the clue for **RAISINY** was 'Often pouring cups one's filled with dried fruit' and **Stephen Fry** discusses the *Times* puzzle in his autobiography *Moab was My Washpot* and the **Scrabble** history is from Paul McCarthy's *Letterati: An Unauthorized Look at Scrabble* ... and, breathe.

**BYGONE:** There is much more on the **history of wordplay** in two authoritative books, *The Oxford Guide to Word Games* by Tony Augarde and C. C. Bombaugh's *Oddities and Curiosities of Words and Literature,* from which some of the examples in this chapter are drawn. **Barbara Hall** is the former crossword editor of the *Sunday Times*; the **RIVER** quote is from the BBC Radio 3 programme *Night Waves*, 13 February 2003. The **SPHINX** clue is from *Guardian* 24,607 by Paul and **CONTINENT** from the 29 June 2012 *New York Times* puzzle. The Rufus clue is from *Guardian* 24,762. The Marcel **Danesi** quotation is from his book *The Puzzle Instinct: The Meaning of Puzzles in Human Life.* The slapdown of **Dame Eleanor Davies** is related in Appleton Morgan's *Macaronic Poetry.* **Lewis Carroll** was the pseudonym of Charles Lutwidge Dodgson, who had toyed with some anagrams for his *nom de guerre*: Edgar U. C. Westhill and Edgar Cuthwellis; the parliamentary anagrams are found in his diary entry for 25 November 1868. The **palindromic clues** are from *Guardian* Quiptic 674 by Orlando and *Guardian* 25,214 by Paul. The rewriting of 'Lewd did I live ...' is from *Language on Vacation: An Olio of Orthographical Oddities* by Dmitri Borgmann.

The '… **pagoda**' palindrome can be found in 'A Day in the Life of Roger Angell', the *New Yorker*, 19 August 1967; **Dan Hoey**'s long one is at *www2.vo.lu/homepages/phahn/anagrams/panama.htm* and Georges **Perec**'s is in the Oulipo collection *La Littérature potentielle: créations, re-créations, récréations*. The acrostic purportedly written by **Queen Victoria** can be found in *Victorian Enigmas* by C. E. Capel. The **NEVA** clues are from *New York Times*, 24 January 2013 by Michael Shteyman and *New York Times*, 6 November 2011 by Elizabeth C. Gorski.

**BEST**: 'Homer and Lisa Exchange Cross Words' is episode six of season twenty. The **Clinton puzzle** is called Twistin' the Oldies and was constructed with Cathy Millhauser and published on 6 May 2007. **Reagle's reminiscences** can be found at his website *sundaycrosswords.com* and in a piece at the *NYT* crossword blog, 'Wordplay: Homer and Lisa Exchange Cross Words' by Jim Horne, 16 November 2008. The remarks on **meh** are from 'Word Featured in *The Simpsons* Becomes Latest Addition to *Collins English Dictionary*', *Daily Telegraph*, 16 November 2008, and there is more on the topic in Stephen Tuohy's piece '¡Ay Caramba! A Look at Some of the Language of *The Simpsons*' at Oxford Dictionaries' *OxfordWords*, 17 April 2013.

**RULED**: **Araucaria**'s thoughts are from the *Guardian*, 20 February 1978, and **Azed**'s are from the *Observer*, 18 February 2001. The 2013 **Azed slip** cited is number 2,126; the slip is available by subscription, at *andlit.org.uk* and at the *Guardian* website. Irish Times Books has collected Crosaire's puzzles in *Crosaire: 120 Crosswords from the* Irish Times.

**TONGUE-TIED**: The '**Gower Street** dialect' is described in *The Slang Dictionary; Or, the Vulgar Words, Street Phrases, and 'Fast'*

*Expressions of High and Low Society*, which has a section on
the related practice of 'back slang', which thieves use to talk
in private: **PENNY** becomes 'yenep', etc. The **Bowra** anecdote
is from his *Memories, 1898–1939* and Spooner's letter from
**Johannesburg** is quoted in William Hayter's *Spooner: A
Biography*. Duchamp's '**eskimo**' phrase can be seen on his
sculpture *Rotary Demisphere (Precision Optics)*, which is in
MoMA, New York. The 'pataphysicist Luc **Étienne**'s book is
called *L'Art du contrepet*, the extract translated by this author,
as are the reminiscences from Gilbert Renault's *Le Livre du
courage et de la peur*. The BBC-approved '**Duce, tes gladiateurs
circulent dans le sang!**' ('Mussolini, your gladiators are blood-
stained') despoonerizes to '*Duce, tes gladiateurs s'enculent
dans le cirque*' (the effect being one akin to 'your gladiators
fuck each other's arses in the circus'), a salty allusion to the
decadent days of Rome. The idea that spoonerisms are not,
in fact, errors is discussed in 'Spoonerisms as Sequencer
Conflicts: Evidence from Artificially Elicited Errors' in the
*American Journal Of Psychology*, 89.3, which also contains
the observation: 'It is almost as if the switching phonemes,
having been driven out of the proper environment, seek the
next best "slot" that is phonologically appropriate, although
this often produces a lexical anomaly.' The gardening
spoonerisms are from season four of the BBC sketch show
the **Two Ronnies**, preceded by a primer on the Revd Spooner
which adds to the attributed lines his advice to a woman that
she would 'soon be had as a matter of course'. **ANTE** is from
Azed 2,006 and **GEMSTONE** is from Azed 1,862.

**SETTLERS**: Afrit's life is described in Derek Harrison's appendix
to his republished edition of *Armchair Crosswords*. The '**Gegs**'

**episode** of *Drop the Dead Donkey* is 'Hoax', the seventh of the second series.

**WHODUNIT**: **Torquemada**'s mystery reviews are listed in William Reynolds's *The Detective Fiction Review of Torquemada: A Selective Index*. **A. J. P. Taylor**'s comments are in *English History 1914–1945* and **A. N. Wilson**'s in *After the Victorians*. Following the Betjeman hoax, Wilson told the *Observer*'s Pendennis (10 September 2006) that he had added 'a short message to previous biographers of my subject hidden in the text of the second printing', adding, 'I won't tell you what it says and couldn't say which page it's on.' The **Stephen Sondheim** comment is from 'How to Do a Real Crossword Puzzle or What's A Four-letter Word for "East Indian Betel Nut" and Who Cares?' in the *New York* magazine, 8 April 1968. In the introduction to Chambers' *Araucaria Crosswords Volume 4*, **Alan Plater** writes that the first thing he and his wife, Shirley, do when the paper arrives is to check whether it's an Araucaria day; Shirley was one of the guests at the ninetieth birthday party for Araucaria, who, following Plater's death in 2010, had produced a tribute puzzle, *Guardian* 25,101. **Colin Dexter**'s news is in the Azed slip 221; Dexter explained the naming of **Morse and Lewis** in the *Observer* article which marked the two-thousandth Azed, 'A Giant among Crosswords', 26 September 2010. Dexter's own puzzles are collected in Chambers' *Morse Crosswords*. The American cryptic definitions are cited by Paul Stynsberg in his collection 'Clever Clue of the Month' at *crosswordese.com*.

**ENIGMA**: **Val Gilbert**'s remarks are from *The Daily Telegraph: 80 Years of Cryptic Crosswords*. **Barbara Hall** was talking to Phillip Dodd for the BBC Radio 3 programme *Night Waves* on 13

February 2003. **Shuchismita Upadhyay** writes *crosswordunclued. com*, probably the most comprehensive and beginner-friendly crossword blog. If you are impressed by Enigma, you should also look at Ross Bereford's Wordplay Wizard.

**ARCANE**: The **vowel data** are from Will Shortz's piece 'What's in a Name? Five Letters or Less', *New York Times*, 9 March 2003. An example of a puzzle where **every answer begins with the same letter** is *Guardian* Genius 66 by Locum and in Anax's *Independent 7,892*, **every clue begins with the word 'is'**. The wartime remarks of Ronald **Carton** are reprinted in *75 Years of the Times Crossword*. The **ILLIN** *New York Times* puzzle was 7 January 2012. **SCREEN** is from *Sunday Telegraph* 2,512 and **CLEAVE** is by Rufus in *Guardian* 24,542. **Peter Piper** is the B-side of 'My Adidas', which is cited in the *Oxford English Dictionary* as an example of 'ill' meaning 'aggressive, irrational, crazy; unpleasant, bad' and the **Fitzgerald** use of 'wicked' is in *This Side of Paradise*. The **Sugarhill Gang** lyric is 'Rapper's Delight'; the **Beastie Boys** rhyme is from 'Rhymin' & Stealin'' and LL Cool J's is 'Fast Peg'.

**HONE**: Kathryn **Friedlander** and Philip Fine's research can be found in 'Expertise in Cryptic Crossword Performance: An Exploratory Survey', presented to the International Symposium on Performance Science and in the forthcoming 'Cryptic Crossword Expertise and Fluid Intelligence'. The **eye-witness** paper is by Michael B. Lewis of Cardiff University. Dr Kathleen Martin Ginis was interviewed about the **'fat'** stories by Hannah Barnes for Radio 5 Live on 5 October 2009. The **negative results** cited are from D. Z. Hambrick, T. A. Salthouse and E. J. Meinz's paper in the *Journal of Experimental Psychology*. Adrian Owen's research into **brain-train programmes** can be found in 'Putting Brain Training to the Test' in *Nature* 465 (published in April 2010). Details of crossword **get-togethers** can be found at *fifteensquared.net*, *bigdave44.com* and *times-xwd-times.livejournal.com*; *crossword.org.uk* has more.

RACY: **GAS** is from *Independent on Sunday* 1,185. **EASED** is from *Telegraph* 26,921; **ELBOW** is from *Guardian* 25,489 by Bonxie and **TRAPEZE** is from *Telegraph* 26,757. Paul's thoughts are in his post 'One's Blue Period' at his blog *Cryptic Crossword Planet*. **STREAKER** is from *Times* Jumbo 985; **DIRTY WEEKEND** is from *Independent* 8,036 and **BUILDER'S BOTTOM** is from *Independent* 7,876. An even more occasional kind of cussing is exemplified by a puzzle published in the *Guardian* by the then-novice setter Paul, in which the answers included, with no further comment, **HORSEMEN, WIDOW TWANKEY, CHARDONNAY, SCUNTHORPE, HOT WATER** and, of course, **MISHIT. SHTUP** is from *FT* 14,242 and the **pink and hard gag** is named by Stephen Fry as 'one of my favourite jokes' in his *Incomplete and Utter History of Classical Music*. Brassless Load is *Listener* 3,285 and Fundamentally Flawed is 3,476, which via Bottom had a Shakespearean aspect to the theme. The '**wanker**' clue is from Azed 1,797. **FANTASTIC** is from *FT* 14,224; **NEWS OF THE WORLD** from *Guardian* 25,408 and **GEORGE BUSH** from *Guardian* 25,008. Francis Wheen's compelling biography is called *Tom Driberg: His Life and Indiscretions*. The definitions of **AARD-ON** and **ZZ BOTTOM** can be found in *Viz*'s seminal reference work *Roger's Profanisaurus*. The **LATIN** clue is by *Times* crossword editor Brian Greer. 'Blue clues? (4)', incidentally, was used by Bonxie in *Guardian* Quiptic 470 to indicate that the answer goes **DOWN**.

# Resources

Citations are mentioned in the notes. The resources I found
most useful and which are most recommended for further
reading are below, in no particular order:

The blogs 'Fifteen Squared', 'Times for the *Times*' and
'Big Dave's Crossword Blog' are of enormous use to
newcomers and, incidentally, the only way of recovering
half-remembered clues and devices.

Don Manley's *Chambers Crossword Manual* is the best
explanation of the innards of puzzles.

*75 Years of the Times Crossword* is an anniversary collection of
puzzles and the reminiscences of editors, setters and
solvers.

*80 Years of the Guardian Cryptic Crossword* is Sandy Balfour's
stocktake of *Guardian* puzzles, setters and culture.

*From Square One: A Meditation, with Digressions, on Crosswords*
is a thoughtful, funny book by Dean Olsher which would
be an excellent read whatever its subject matter.

*Crossword Puzzles: Their History and Their Cult*: Roger
  Millington's rambunctious tour through the state of
  crosswording circa 1974.
Georges Perec's *Les Mots croisés, procédés de considérations de
  l'auteur sur l'art et la manière de croiser les mots*: the playful
  Frenchman's philosophy of puzzling.
Tony Augarde's *Oxford Guide to Word Games*, which also has
  chapters on letter games, alphabet games, Scrabble …
*Wordplay* (2006): Patrick Creadon and Christine O'Malley's
  documentary about American puzzlers.
*Timeshift: How to Solve a Cryptic Crossword* (2008): Georgina
  Harvey's BBC documentary about the UK cryptic scene.

# Acknowledgements

This book relied on the help of many superb people:

All those with whom I learned to solve, including my brother Alexander, my late dad, Shaun Pye, Charlie Rowlands, Sean Walsh, Mark Chappell and Lucy Brett.

Those who have given this book its structure: Araucaria for writing the clues in the puzzle at the beginning of this book, Rufus for the title, and Denise Sutherland for the index.

The setters who have guided me through their world including Enigmatist, Paul, Arachne, Monk, Azed, Tramp, Orlando, Puck, Shed, Brendan Emmett Quigley, Audreus, Gordius, Micawber, Goujeers, Trazom, Hot and Philistine.

Those who have provided information and wisdom, including Sean Walsh, David Bellos, Kathryn Friedlander, Noah Veltman, Anne R. Bradford, Richard Browne, Mike Hutchinson, Peter Biddlecombe, Will Shortz, Evie Eysenburg, Nitsuh Abebe, Shuchi Upadhyay, Deb Ablem, Jane Teather, Charlotte Murray, Brendan Carr, Jean Valentine, Laura Cremer, Stephan

Shakespeare, Faria Iqbal, Jane Sewell, Michael Price, Julian Mitchell and Colin Dexter – and Eric Westbrook and Jerry Farrell for their puzzles.

The staff of Caffè Torelli in Kew, for enduring the man in the corner surrounded by yellowing newspapers and books.

Janine Gibson of the *Guardian* for sharing my enthusiasm for editorial around puzzles, that paper's crossword editor Hugh Stephenson, the editing team at *Guardian* Life & Style – Kate Carter, Rachel Dixon and Rachel Holmes – and the readers of and commenters at the 'Guardian *Crossword Blog*'.

Those who enabled this book to sit in your hands: my agent Andrew Gordon and editor Helen Conford, Giles Wilson for facilitating and the Penguin team for their ideas and encouragement, including Sarah Day, Rose Goddard, Rebecca Lee, Ingrid Matts, Stefan McGrath, Natalie Ramm and Kate Watson.

For feeding and watering my playing with words: my English teacher Kenneth Fitzell and my mum.

For waiting: Lucy and Raphael.

# Index

Notes: For names starting with 'The', search on the second word. Cryptic clues to solve are set in **bold**.